D0095209

MIRACLES
of Healing

WHEN MIRACLES HAPPEN
True Stories of God's Divine Touch

Edited by Phyllis Hobe

Guideposts Books
Carmel, New York

234.131
MIR

Acknowledgments

Every attempt has been made to credit the sources of copyrighted material used in this book. If any such acknowledgment has been inadvertently omitted or miscredited, receipt of such information would be appreciated.

Scripture quotations marked (KJV) are taken from *The King James Version of the Bible.*

Scripture quotations marked (NIV) are taken from *The Holy Bible*, New International Version. Copyright © 1973, 1978, 1984, International Bible Society. Used by permission of Zondervan Bible Publishers.

Scripture quotations marked (TLB) are taken from *The Living Bible*. Copyright © 1971 by Tyndale House Publishers, Wheaton, IL 60187. All rights reserved.

"Look, Mom, It's Gone," by Cheryl Gade, and "The God Who Heals," by Elroy (Al) Plue, are from *Miracles Still Happen*, published by Harrison House, Inc., used by permission. "Unconditional Love," by Jean Martin, "We're Trying, God," by Judie Gulley, "A Gift of Love," by Margaret Cheasebro, "The Pitch," by Jim McElhatton, and "Unmeasurable Miracle," by Ann J. Brady, are published by permission from from *Whispers From Heaven*, Copyright © 2002, 2003 Publications International, LTD. "In Need of a Friend" is from *A Treasury of Miracles for Friends*, by Karen Kingsbury, Copyright © 2004, by Karen Kingsbury, published by Warner Books, Inc., used by permission. "The Wedding," by John P. Walker, is from *God Allows U-Turns*, by Allison Gappa Bottke with Cheryl Hutchings and Ellen Regan, Copyright © 2001, by Allison Gappa Bottke, published by Promise Press, used by permission; "The Gift of Dance," is from *A Treasury of Miracles for Women*, by Karen Kingsbury, Copyright © 2002, by Karen Kingsbury, published by Warner Books, Inc., used by permission.

"Some Pennies Really Might Be From Heaven," by Phyllis Edgerly; "Bluebirds for Bailey," by Anne Culbreath Watkins; "The Moose and a Miracle," by Kerry Sprague; "The Power of Prayer," by Betty R. Graham; "Finding the Strength to Overcome," by Renie Szilak Burghardt; "Painting Life by Numbers," by Kathryn Lay; "You Must Be Brave," by Carla Zwahlen; "Silent Treatment," by Kathy Mattea; "The Healing," by Pat MeHaffey; "The Messenger," by Lonnie Hull DuPont; "More Than a Thousand Words," by Donna Lowich; "Suffer the Little Children," by Lenora Hite; "The Car Ride," by Betty R. Graham; "The Sign of the Rose," by Kristyna Szajowska; "Someone Watching Over Us," by Donna Lowich; "Every Knee Shall Bow," by Diane M. Ciarloni; "The Ice Storm," by Bob Bedore; "God's Network," by Rachael Phillips; "A Divine Detour," by Lynn Seely; "House Call," by T. J. Banks; "Alone," by Lynn Seely; "I Don't Want to Be Angry," by Kathryn Lay; are used by permission of the authors.

www.guideposts.org
(800) 431-2344
Guideposts Books & Inspirational Media Division

Designed by Rittenhouse Graphics
Illustrations by Ron Bucalo
Cover photo © Royalty-Free/Corbis
Jacket designed by The DesignWorks Group

Printed in the United States of America

Contents

CHAPTER 2 FACING OUR FEARS

∼∼∼

*C*HAPTER 3   THE COMFORT OF MEMORIES

≋≋

CHAPTER 4   WHEN GOD INTERVENES

*C*HAPTER 5   NEW PATHS TO FOLLOW

Introduction

How often we speak of miracles, and yet not really know what they are? Wishes fulfilled? Help when we need it? Comfort when we're hurt? Guidance when we've lost our way? All of the above? Miracles are limited only by our own imaginations, not God's, Who uses them to remind us that He is present in our lives at all times.

We experience miracles in many different ways. Some are ordinary events and some are life-changing moments. Some come to us through other people—family, friends, even strangers—and some come directly—and unmistakably—from God. There are miracles in every life.

The stories in *Miracles of Healing* are written by men and women who have had to face serious illnesses and threats to their lives. When there isn't always a cure, we may need a miracle to strengthen our faith that God is by our side.

In the first chapter, "Living With Hope", a little boy's brothers and parents come together at his bedside to help prepare him for the surgery that might save his life. A daughter is comforted by the reassurance of her deceased mother that her father will recover from his illness. A wife and mother is overwhelmed by a diagnosis of diabetes and prays that it is a mistake.

Life can be very frightening, and in "Facing Our Fears" we read stories of people who are more threatened by their reaction to a situation than the situation itself. A woman suffering severe depression struggles to overcome thoughts of suicide. A young wife in wartime grapples with the fear that her husband is in danger. The mother of a recovering alcoholic son cannot sleep when he does not come home.

In "The Comfort of Memories", you'll read stories of people who have lost loved ones and are trying to deal with their grief. A woman whose mother suffered a long illness is comforted by a dream assuring her that her mother is in Heaven. A reporter who mourns the loss of his brother in an automobile accident recalls the joy of the many ballgames they played together. A mother faced with a long recovery from paralysis finds strength and encouragement from snapshots of her children.

The stories in Chapter 4, "When God Intervenes", describe life-changing miracles that lead us to faith. A woman who doubts the existence of God finds an end to her physical pain as she discovers Him. A man whose wife is dangerously ill calls upon God to lead them through a furious storm to a place where she can be helped. A woman who loses her way along a familiar road realizes that God had an important reason for the unexpected detour.

A very important part of healing is the ability to go on with a life that has been interrupted. In "New Paths to Follow", God uses miracles to guide people into unfamiliar but helpful ways. A young widow with a child moves from the house where she and her husband lived to one that needs her care, and in the process finds that she can survive. A caring woman with a fierce temper takes on the challenge to become the person God wants her to be. A veteran facing surgery with a poor chance of survival comes to terms with a doctor who believes his faith will make the difference.

All of the stories in this book are true. All of the miracles happened. And all of them tell us that we are loved by a God who cares about us every moment of our lives.

PHYLLIS HOBE

MIRACLES
of Healing

CHAPTER 1

Living With Hope

We have this hope as an anchor for the soul, firm and secure. It enters the inner sanctuary behind the curtain, where Jesus, who went before us, has entered on our behalf... (Hebrews 6:19–20, NIV).

When we know that God is near, that He is always ready to walk with us through the darkest hours, we have hope. The outcome may not be what we wish, but we can be certain that we will not have to face it alone. We can yield to God's will because we know that He knows what is best for us and those we love.

Look, Mom, It's Gone

CHERYL GADE

In 1993 we had moved from Minnesota to Spokane, Washington, after my husband accepted a management position at a craft store. Our first summer was filled with getting our new house in order, finding a school for the boys, and locating a good church.

The bold messages taught by our new pastor caused us to act on our beliefs and be "doers" of the Word (James 1:22). Faith seemed new and fresh to us as we discovered a deeper walk with God.

Bedtime has always been precious to our family. One storybook often turned into two or three. After reading a Bible story, the boys cleverly offered their personal translation of the story by adding unique details. Sweet voices prayed for blessings, hugs and kisses were shared, little bodies were tucked in, and the lights were turned off.

One night, while kissing my youngest cherub, Douglas, I noticed a bubble at the base of his teeth. With the growing experience of raising three rambunctious boys, I did not panic over the unexpected find but decided to keep an eye on the growth that made its home in my son's mouth.

I examined Douglas's mouth nightly. The bubble consistently grew until it caused his lip to protrude. We questioned him with growing concern. "Does it hurt? Can you move it with your tongue? Does it bother you?"

Douglas had developed into a "tough" little boy by having two older brothers. Though only three, he knew how to handle the rough stuff. Ear infections never bothered him and fever did not slow him down. This new challenge provoked no bother or worry to my young lad. I, on the other hand, was concerned enough to pursue a solution.

Being new to the city, we asked around to locate a trustworthy dentist. After a quick examination, we were ushered into the dentist's office. "I've never seen anything like this before," the doctor said with concern.

We were immediately referred to another dentist who could surgically remove the growth. They planned to anesthetize Douglas, then biopsy the bubble once it was removed.

My thoughts reeled. He's only three, Lord. I don't want him to have surgery. We didn't even have insurance yet. Gathering up my innocent child, who knew nothing of the fear that descended on his mother, we headed to see his father at work.

My detailed report to Scott was solemn. "Call and schedule the surgery," he offered as a logical conclusion. "We have to get this taken care of." I knew Scott well enough to realize he was equally concerned about Douglas, yet he stood strong to carry me through my weak moment.

Hearing our dilemma, the assistant manager spoke up, "Well, we'll just believe that he'll be fine, in Jesus' name. God will take good care of him!"

We stared at her in wonderment. Faith! I was quickly reminded that faith was more powerful than any sickness or disease that would attempt to place itself on our child.

That night, bedtime was sweet as always. However, after the Bible story, Scott took control of our prayer time. "We're going to pray for Douglas's mouth," he said with authority.

We had learned from the scripture that if someone was sick, we could lay hands on him and pray in faith for his healing. Douglas's two older brothers bounded out of bed, jumped onto Douglas's bed, and laid their little hands on their brother. Scott placed his hand on his chin and prayed a simple prayer of faith while I stroked his hair. After hugs and kisses, the boys jumped back into their beds, and the lights went out.

The next day was bright and sunny. Waking the boys, I took a few minutes to rub backs and tousle hair.

When Douglas welcomed me with a bear hug, I quickly asked him if I could look inside his mouth as I had done each morning for many days.

Douglas dutifully pulled down his lip on one side, revealing a pink, healthy gum line. Hmm, I thought. It must be the other side. He pulled down the lip on the other side. I saw nothing.

"Douglas, open your mouth wide," I commanded. Inspecting his mouth as a buyer would inspect a horse, I found no abrasion, scar, or redness, only clear, pink gum tissue. The ugly looking bubble had completely disappeared.

Smothering my baby with hugs as he squirmed to get loose, I celebrated our miracle. Douglas's attention was already focused on breakfast.

Unconditional Love

JEAN MARTIN

Throughout my life, my mother has been my biggest fan—she always told me I was beautiful, smart, and talented. Even as an adult, when I was working as a teacher and would meet my mother for lunch every day, I could count on having my ego stroked and my self-confidence increased. Mother listened with rapt attention to everything I said, knew just what to do to encourage me, and always offered support.

But then I began to notice changes in my mother. They were so subtle at first that only I, who saw her every day, noticed them. Her cheerful, optimistic attitude was replaced by suspicion and fear. Her interest in her appearance diminished, and I often found her at lunch dressed in dirty, torn blouses. Her conversations became self-centered and filled with paranoid fears concerning her house, her money, and people in her life.

I was so concerned about her personality change, I got my mother to visit a doctor. He diagnosed her as having advancing dementia. I was devastated. As the months passed, my mother's short-term memory diminished, and she became a person who either lived in the past or centered on the immediate moment, forgetting what had transpired only hours or minutes before. I mourned the loss of my nurturing mother, and felt little joy in visiting her and undertaking the new responsibilities of caring for her. The God my mother prayed to every day seemed to have forgotten her. Visits to her became sad parts of my daily routine, and I longed for a return to happier times.

One night as I lay on my couch at home, the telephone rang. My mother's neighbor reported that my mother had fallen and was lying on the living-room floor in obvious distress. She was taken to the hospital and X rayed. Her left shoulder and back had been seriously bruised. Her mobility was greatly reduced, and she had to remain in the hospital. This was all very confusing for a lady suffering from severe dementia. Each day was like torture to her, as she felt her family had abandoned her to the care of others.

I realized that leaving Mother in the hospital was not helping her, so I took a leave of absence from my teaching position and brought her home. Those first days were horrible. She was confused about where she was and often called me "nurse." Her mind frequently wandered to the past. While it was frustrating for me initially, I soon realized that it allowed me to see parts of my mother's life I had never known before.

At times, she thought she was still married to her first husband, Freddy, and I listened as she recounted what it was like to be a young bride during World War II, married to a sailor on convoy duty. She worried about him, but said giving birth to his son was a great joy in her life. She sadly recounted how Freddy only saw Teddy, their son, on a brief visit before he had to return to duty. She was eagerly awaiting his return when the devastating telegram arrived—he had been killed while crossing the North Atlantic. She was alone with their son but faced her new life bravely. She found joy in her son and, with her resilient, resourceful nature, conquered her grief and raised her son for ten years on her own. She gave to him what she gave to me: nurturing love, undivided attention, unwavering support, and enthusiastic encouragement.

Gradually, I found myself giving those very gifts back to my mother. My depression melted away, and I started to cherish the time I got to spend with her, reliving her life through memories and becoming her biggest supporter.

To my great joy, she was eventually able to get up from chairs and her bed independently. We celebrated every achievement. When she remembered what day of the week it was, we rejoiced, and if she forgot what street she lived on, we meandered down memory lane, and she spoke of all the places she had lived. This lessened her anxiety and eventually allowed her to recall her life with me.

I realized at last what my mother had understood so long ago: the power of unconditional love. It was the love she had given to me all my life; the love I gradually learned to return to her. I knew that such a love could exist, especially with God's help, and it was through my mother that I learned how to make that love a reality.

Some Pennies Really Might Be From Heaven

PHYLLIS EDGERLY

For nearly twenty years, my father has headed south, like so many other birds of "the Greatest Generation." As soon as New England leaves begin taking on their autumn finery, he packs up his car with its Florida license plate, dodges the worst of hurricane season, and makes his way back to the land of orange groves and flamingos.

But this year was different. First there were the meteorological monsters that never stopped coming to the Florida area. And then there was his own personal storm—cancer—that has changed so many of his plans lately. For the first time in my adult life, Dad stayed in New England for most of a fall season. It was late enough in the year that folks were already asking him about his plans for Thanksgiving and Christmas. And it was early enough in his battle with disease that he was still tentative about making plans of any sort.

It was also five years after my mother's death and I

couldn't help remembering a little miracle that had occurred during that first lonely holiday season he had faced on his own. Without his companion of six decades, he had been the very embodiment of sadness.

Within a week of her death, he had collapsed and been hospitalized. When I flew down to see him I knew that, regardless of his illness, he was really fighting to find the will to live, and might not succeed. By the time Christmas carols were playing on my rental-car radio, Dad had become increasingly unresponsive, and my heart sank heavier each day.

I remember saying prayers one night that smacked of desperation, pleading, and outright bargaining. I also remember the fear I had that I was going to lose both of my parents even before I'd begun to thaw from the numbness of my mother's death. She seemed as far away for me as he did, lying helplessly in his hospital bed, and I felt very alone.

When I could finally allow my thoughts to quiet a bit that night, I felt a sensation like a soft hand placed briefly on my shoulder, then experienced a feeling similar to what I'd felt in the past when my mother would so often urge, "Come on, Pet—it'll be all right," whenever I'd shared my troubles with her.

That feeling finally allowed me to go to sleep. Then I had a dream that I was standing in the doorway of my Dad's hospital bathroom, watching as he stood at the sink with his back to me. Someone was standing behind him, much the way a nurse would do, to steady and support him. When I looked in the mirror over the sink, I saw that it was my mother who was standing behind him. Her eyes immediately looked up and gazed back at me before the dream ended.

The next morning, when I went to see Dad at the hospital, a nurse stopped me on my way to his room to advise that he had gotten up in the night without assistance and, fortunately, made his way to the bathroom without incident. While she was unhappy about his method, she was obviously glad to share news of his improved circumstances after he'd lain immobile in bed for nearly two weeks. He had also taken not one, but two walks that morning, she told me.

If my expression was astonished, Dad's was positively ecstatic when I came upon him sitting up in his room. He couldn't wait to tell me about his "coup" of getting up and walking all that way. He hadn't actually wanted to do it at first, he told me, but "your mother simply insisted, and so I just had to comply."

After he'd said those words, he looked a bit abashed, as though he regretted letting them out, in case I'd think he was crazy. I'm sure that I must have looked a bit dazed myself, standing there staring at him with my mouth open.

We've never spoken of it since, although over the

last five years he periodically mentions curious little coincidences that help me feel that my mother is near, and leave him absolutely assured that she is.

The latest happened as he was gathering up his things before we headed over to the first of many radiation treatments that he would receive. He noticed something on the carpet in his living room and stooped down to retrieve it. It was a penny, something that my mother, like many people, always considered a sign of good luck.

Only this penny, or "pence," had Queen Elizabeth on the front—like those my English mother so often carried in her pocket. Dad hadn't seen one around the house for years.

But I have no doubt that it's been in his own pocket ever since.

Brought Together

ALLEN VAN METER

"God, please, no!" I wanted to cry out that night when my sister called and told me what happened to my nephew, Michael. He had suffered a gunshot wound to the head. A careless accident, but the damage was massive and irreversible. Only machines were keeping him alive. "Come home," my sister whispered as she hung up. "Help us." I would have done anything for her and Michael, but even as my wife, Marilyn, grabbed the phone and started calling airlines, trying to get us seats on the next flight to Kentucky, I couldn't quite bring myself to believe he was gone.

Michael was my sister's son. His father wasn't in the picture, so I was the one who looked out for him and took him fishing when he was little. I tried so hard to protect him from the rough-and-tumble life of the Kentucky backwoods, the life that would have destroyed me if the Lord hadn't come to my rescue. I'd even had Michael live with Marilyn and me in Florida when his teenage rebelliousness got to be too much for my sister to handle. He was a lot like me, the good and the bad. Hard-headed yet big-hearted, a taste for living on the edge mixed with a bedrock belief in the value of hard work. Both Michael and I grew a lot in those years together—he because our boys looked up to him like a big brother, I because I knew he was looking to me for an example.

Memories played through my mind like an old, grainy home movie. Little Michael jumping up and down with his first catch from the creek. Michael gleefully (and skillfully) driving a front loader before he was old enough to get his learner's permit. Michael working three jobs at once, then zooming around on his motorcycle after hours. Michael calling us just a few days ago so excited, like a kid on Christmas morning, about finding God. He was only twenty-five. How could it all be taken away from him in a single senseless moment? Lord, this doesn't make sense, I prayed. You gave me a second chance. Why not Michael?

Really, my turnaround was nothing short of a miracle. Back then, I was totally broken from my addictions to alcohol and drugs. The crime I'd turned to in order to support my habit landed me in a Florida prison and forced me to dry out, but it didn't do anything for the self-destructive spiral I was continuing down.

One day in early 1989 I was slumped on my bunk in my cell, thinking, I've messed up everything worth caring about. I might as well be dead. Then a fellow inmate came by. "I'm going to chapel," he said. "You're coming with me." I couldn't muster the energy to argue, so I followed him out of the cell block. I sat way in the back of the chapel like a zombie, not even caring where I was.

All of sudden a presence spoke to me, the voice cutting clear through my despair. "Allen, if you give Me your life, I'll restore it back to you." I knew it could only be God. Who else could bring a spiritually dead man back to life?

The rest of my sentence I read the Bible and got to know the Lord. I talked to Him like I'd talk to a friend. "God, let me know what You want me to do," I'd ask. "I'm kind of thick-headed, so You'll probably have to speak real loud and clear to get through to me."

One morning that spring, I was lying on my bunk with my Bible open on my chest, thinking about my release in September. Again, I felt the presence I'd felt in chapel and heard a direct message: "Wait until after February 14 to get married. I will bring her to you." That sure came out of the blue! I hadn't given marriage much thought because I figured it would be next to impossible to find a woman willing to share her life with someone who'd messed up his own so bad. I tucked that promise from God away in the back of my mind. First things first, I figured. I was released and went into an aftercare center in Jacksonville, Florida.

I was at an evening service at the church down the

road the Sunday after Valentine's Day 1990, sitting in the same pew as two little boys, unable to take my eyes off the blond leading the songs. I'd noticed her that morning at coffee hour, too. Marilyn, the preacher said her name was. She's the one, something kept telling me. The singing ended. She came down the aisle and sat down—right in my pew, between me and the boys. She was their mom. The service went on, and the younger boy nodded off. Pretty soon he was stretched out on the pew fast asleep, scooting his mom right up next to me. That was the confirmation I needed. I worked up my nerve and asked Marilyn out for coffee the next night. Not long after that, I asked her to be my wife. Turned out Marilyn, too, had felt the Lord leading us together.

In the ten years since our marriage, we hadn't been apart, and it was at moments like tonight, facing this tragedy in my family, that I was most grateful God had given me Marilyn to lean on.

She hung up the telephone. "Finally, some good news," she said. "I got you on a flight leaving first thing in the morning. You'll change planes in Memphis—"

"Wait," I interrupted her, confused, "aren't you coming with me?"

"There's only one seat left on that plane," she said. "You need to be in it. I'll take a later flight." She must have seen my look of dismay. "Don't worry, Allen, I'll be right behind you."

Right behind me, Lord? I need Marilyn right there next to me!

The phone rang before I could say anything. "The doctors said Michael's brain-dead. They're asking me to donate his organs," my sister sobbed. "Please make the decision. I just can't."

"Donating would be the right thing to do," I said slowly. "At least some good can come out of this. Hang on. I'll be there tomorrow."

Early the following morning Marilyn dropped me off at the airport. I picked up my ticket and went to the gate. "Sir, you're seated in 8B, on the aisle," the flight attendant said. Lord, I'm leaning on You like always. Tell me what to do. I'll do it. I promise.

At row 8, a dark-haired woman in a red blazer was trying to get her suitcase into the overhead bin. I gave her a hand. She nodded her thanks, then wordlessly settled into the window seat.

Shortly after takeoff, she pulled some papers out of her purse and studied them intently. I glanced over. They were diagrams of the human body. Maybe she could answer some of my questions about Michael. "Excuse me," I said, "are you a doctor?"

"No," she sighed. "I'm going over these because my sister's in bad shape, and she needs one of my kidneys."

"I'm sorry to hear that," I said.

"Debbie's been sick for a long time," she said.

"With liver disease, actually. She got a transplant, only now her body's rejecting it. She's on the waiting list for another liver, but all the medication she's taking has damaged her kidneys. I'm on my way to her hospital in New Orleans to get tested as a donor."

"I'm headed to Kentucky because my family's going through something similar," I said. "My nephew is being taken off life support. We're going to donate his organs."

"It was good of your family to make the decision to donate."

She went back to her medical diagrams, and I closed my eyes to get some rest. But my mind kept going back to another conversation, the last one I had with Michael. He'd been so awestruck at finding God at work in his life.

God at work...My eyes flew open. I tapped my seatmate on the shoulder. "I think there's a reason we ended up next to each other. I have a feeling my nephew's liver should go to your sister." As soon as I said that, I sensed the Lord's presence, as real and unmistakable as I had those other times, telling me, Yes, this is what I want you to do.

"It's not that simple," my seatmate said. "There are all kinds of rules. And the blood and tissue types must match."

I stared at the air phone in the seatback before us,

the voice of the Lord resounding in my head: This is what I want you to do. "Look, it's more than coincidence," I insisted. "This is definitely God at work here. I feel it. We have to get on that phone right now and find out how to get the liver to your sister."

This time my seatmate didn't argue. She dug out a credit card and a list of numbers, and punched one into the air phone. "This is Jan Larson," she said. "My sister, Deborah White, is on your waiting list for a liver transplant." Jan explained what we were looking to do and listened for a while to the response. Then she turned to me. "The nurse says we can do this. It's called a directed donation. They'll still have to confirm the organ match and be able to get it to New Orleans within ten hours. Can you call the hospital where your nephew is and get things started there?"

I picked up the air phone, dialed and got through to the transplant coordinator. "My name is Allen Van Meter. My nephew is Michael Gibson. He was declared brain-dead not long ago, and his mother signed the papers to donate his organs. Well, we have a woman in New Orleans we want to give his liver to."

"I'm sorry," the nurse said. "It's too late. They're about to unhook Michael and wheel him into the O.R. to harvest his organs."

"This is of God!" I practically shouted. "It's not too late!"

Silence. Then I heard the phone being set down and footsteps scurrying away. It seemed like forever before the nurse got back on the line. "It wasn't too late," she said quietly. "I stopped them."

"Jan, we're just in time!" I exclaimed.

At the Memphis airport, Jan and I exchanged numbers. "I can't tell you how much your nephew's gift means. Please thank your sister," she said. "We'll pray for you." She gave me a big hug good-bye, and rushed to catch her connecting flight to New Orleans.

Three days later, I was struggling over Michael's eulogy, Marilyn at my side again, when Jan called from New Orleans. "Debbie's doing great," she said. "Your nephew's liver really and truly came just in time." She explained that during the operation, the surgeons discovered Debbie's hepatic artery—the main blood line to the liver—was so clogged that she had only hours to live. If they'd gone ahead with just the kidney transplant as planned, it would have killed her. "Even the doctors say it's a miracle. Debbie was in intensive care for weeks after her first liver transplant. This time she's doing so well that pretty soon she'll be coming to thank you in person. She's been telling everyone Michael and the Lord turned the sunset of her life into a glorious sunrise."

I knew what I would say at Michael's funeral. I would talk about one of his kidneys going to a young father; the other to a little boy. A three-month-old baby got his corneas; a badly burned child, skin grafts. Fifty cancer patients received some of his bone marrow. And, of course, I would tell everyone about how I ended up with the last seat left on that plane, right next to a woman whose sister was in dire need of a transplant. It was all because of the One who helped my family make sense of our tragedy by transforming it into a second chance for so many others.

Bluebirds for Bailey

ANNE CULBREATH WATKINS

At first glance, I fell head over heels in love with the squirming, squalling baby boy lying on my daughter's tummy. Joyful tears cascaded down my cheeks as I gazed at him, not only because he was my firstborn grandchild, but because Bailey's arrival was nothing short of a miracle.

His birth signaled the end of eight-and-a-half tense months of constant prayers for Laura and the developing fetus. As an insulin-dependent diabetic, Laura had faced the prospects of giving birth to a less-than-healthy and possibly even stillborn infant. And now there he lay, perfectly formed from the top of his head to the tips of his ten tiny toenails. I had never felt more blessed! But a week later, terror dimmed my joy when Bailey began to experience brief, strange episodes of jerky movements.

Believing that the episodes were seizures, his doctor said that Bailey would need to see a pediatric neurologist. Kindly, he called to set up an appointment and informed us that until the scheduled visit, we were to keep a close eye on Bailey and note the times and durations of any further episodes.

My daughter and her husband were horribly frightened, and I was frightened for them as well as for my precious little grandson. Would he need harsh seizure medications? Had he suffered brain damage after all? Trembling with fear, I drove home from the emergency room, every breath I drew holding a prayer for Bailey.

Early the morning of his appointment, I settled by the telephone to wait for news. But soon, consumed by the same choking sense of dread that had overwhelmed me since his first mysterious episode, I found myself pacing back and forth, unable to stop my flood of tears.

After awhile, I needed to get out of the house for a few minutes and decided to walk up to the mailbox. Grabbing the portable telephone, I stuck it in my pocket and headed out the door. It was an odd, spring-like day and very mild for February. Brilliant sunshine drenched the surrounding fields but, heavyhearted, I barely noticed.

On the way, a bright bluebird fluttered across the path in front of me. Giving it a brief glance, I continued to trudge along, too engulfed in fear to care. I collected the mail and headed back to the house. Another bluebird surprised me by landing in the path, and this one seemed determined to get my attention. It hopped along the ground in front of me, and then took flight.

Several more joined the first and soon a big bunch of bluebirds was cavorting and wheeling before me.

I stopped walking and gasped in amazement. What in the world was a whole flock of bluebirds doing, playing around like that in the middle of the driveway? As I watched, I became aware of a sudden lightness to my body, as if an oppressive, heavy burden had physically lifted from my shoulders. For the first time in days, I felt a sense of hopefulness. Could those bluebirds be trying to tell me something? My feet barely touched the ground as I hurried to the house.

I dragged a seat around on the front porch and deposited the telephone on the chair arm beside me. A warm patch of sun fell over me, and as I watched the birds, I basked in a soothing pool of calmness. Then the telephone rang. I whispered a quick prayer and said hello.

"Mom!" Laura's voice sounded tired, but happy. "The doctor finished the first round of tests and said Bailey looks fine—he didn't find any problems!"

This time, the tears that sprang to my eyes were tears of joy. Smiling, I listened as Laura continued. "They're going to run an EEG and then we can come home."

She promised to call me as soon as she had more news, and we hung up. As I waited for the next telephone call, I continued to pray for Bailey, but this time it was with a lovely sense of peace.

After the EEG, the neurologist told Laura that there were no signs of brain damage, and that Bailey was a healthy, perfect baby. He couldn't explain what had happened, but speculated that the odd episodes might have been caused by low blood sugars. The huge amounts of insulin Laura required while pregnant had not only lowered her blood sugars, but the baby's, as well. Thankfully, no follow up visits to the neurologist would be necessary. Best of all, Bailey wouldn't need to take any seizure medications.

My heart sang as I thanked God for Bailey's miracle. At the same time, I praised Him for caring enough about a worried grandma to send those beautiful little bluebirds to be messengers of encouragement and cheer.

A miracle and a personal message from God, all in the same day; what more could I ask?

In Need of a Friend

KAREN KINGSBURY

Bonner Davis knew the end was near, but he could do nothing to change his situation. He had advanced throat cancer, mounting medical bills, and no way to pay for the experimental treatment that could save his life.

A retired forest ranger, Bonner and his wife, Angela, lived in North Carolina where they existed on his meager pension and a faith bigger than the Smoky Mountains. Once in a while, Bonner would share his fears with Angela. She was his best friend, and though he looked forward to Heaven, he didn't want to leave her.

Angela's answer was always the same. "God knows what we need, Bonner. I'm praying for a miracle and, somehow, somehow, I believe He'll give us one."

In nearby Spartanburg, millionaire Olsen Matthews was celebrating his sixtieth birthday. Single, and without any close friends, Olsen chose to spend his day in the air. He was a novice pilot who always felt more complete when he was alone in his small Cessna plane.

Sunshine reigned that afternoon, and Olsen savored

the familiar rush as he took to the air. He'd been in the air twenty minutes when the rush faded to a sort of soul-searching, which often happened when Olsen flew. What was life about, anyway? He had more money than he knew what to do with, but not a single person he could call a friend. Sure, Olsen had advisors and peers he did business with. But he had no family, no friend who cared about him.

This time as he flew, gazing down at the rolling hills and valleys, another thought filled Olsen's heart: What about God? All his life he'd denied the idea of both creation and Creator, but now, with his life waning toward the sunset years, he sometimes wondered.

What if God was real? What if he had a few things to do before he died in order to be right with that God? The possibility set his nerves on edge and made him wish once more for a friend, someone he could share his thoughts with. Perhaps even someone who knew something about God and why so many people believed in Him.

Olsen was about to turn his plane around and soar back over the mountains when he heard a sharp pop. At the same instant, the engine cut out. Olsen felt a wave of adrenaline rush through his veins, but he stayed calm. He'd never lost an engine before, but there were ways to handle the situation. He flipped a series of switches designed to restart the motor, but none of them worked.

Okay, he told himself, time for Plan B.

If the engine wouldn't reengage, Olsen's only hope was to glide the plane in lazy circles toward the ground and make an emergency landing. By using the wing flaps and other instruments, he could slow the speed of the aircraft and still walk away. At the same time, the plane could catch a wrong current and plummet to the ground.

"God!" He called the name out loud, and he heard the fear in his voice. "If You're real, help me. I'm not ready to go."

Two minutes passed in textbook fashion, but then, as Olsen had feared, a strong current dropped the right wing of the plane and the craft began to tumble. Olsen had another thousand feet to go before hitting land, but as the plane fell he spotted a lake. Water, he thought. That's my only hope. Landing in the trees or on the hilly ground would cause the Cessna to disintegrate on impact.

"Water. God, if You're listening, lead me to the water."

The ground was rushing up to meet him. Suddenly his plane fell to the left and Olsen could see he was going to hit the small lake. The last thing he remembered was the sound of water breaking over his plane and the rush of ice-cold wetness filling the cabin. Suddenly the craft jolted to a stop and Olsen smacked his head on the doorframe.

After that, there was only darkness.

Bonner was pouring himself a glass of iced tea when he saw a small plane tumble into view and freefall into the lake at the edge of his property.

"Angela, quick! Call 9-1-1. A plane just crashed into the lake."

After years of outdoor training and living, Bonner had always been in good shape. But the cancer medication had taken its toll, and as he ran toward the lake he could barely catch his breath. Fifty yards, a hundred, two hundred, and finally he reached the shore.

The situation was more grim than he'd thought.

The wing of the plane jutted out of the water, but it was otherwise buried in a section of the lake some ten feet deep and seventy-five yards off shore. No one else must have seen the crash, because he was the only one standing at the water's edge looking for signs of life. His heart raced within him, and he still hadn't caught his breath. But he had no choice. Whoever was in the plane was drowning even at that very moment. Before he jumped in, he uttered a silent prayer: *God, if I don't make it back to shore, let Angela know how much I love her.*

Then he dove in and headed as hard and fast as he could toward the plane. Because of his weakened condition, the swim took Bonner twice as long as it normally would have. After five minutes, he reached the wing and though his lungs were already burning from the effort, he sucked in as much air as he could and dove down. His heart pounded, filling his senses with an urgency that drove him deep, deeper toward the fuselage door. He tried twice to open it, and finally on the third try, the door swung free.

Bonner was out of air.

He swam to the surface, nauseated from the effort, grabbed another breath, and went back down. This time he found the pilot in seconds and felt around until he was sure the person was alone. Feeling as though he could die at any moment, Bonner dragged the unconscious man to the surface. They weren't out of danger yet, and that terrified Bonner because, simply, he was out of energy.

Help me, God. Help me. Bonner let the words play in his mind again and again as he kept himself and the man afloat. It took no time to realize that the pilot wasn't breathing.

Swimming with a strength that wasn't his own, Bonner dragged the pilot back to shore. On the beach, despite his exhaustion, he managed to administer CPR. He was three minutes into the process when an emergency crew arrived and took over. He barely made it to the edge of a grove of trees before he dropped to the ground, unable to go on.

At almost the same time, Angela came running toward him. "Bonner!" She waved down one of the paramedics and Bonner heard her explain about his cancer. "Help him, please."

The emergency worker moved quickly and hooked Bonner up to intravenous fluids. They took him to the local hospital, and four hours later he was ready to go home. Before he left, he heard the news about the pilot. The CPR had saved his life.

Bonner figured that might be the end of the situation, but the next day he received a visit from the pilot.

"My name's Olsen Matthews. You saved my life." The man shook Bonner's hand. "The paramedics said you were praying out loud, thanking God at the scene."

"Yes." Bonner stared at the man. He looked wonderful, considering he should have died in the plane crash. "My wife and I were both praying."

The man's eyes grew watery. "Thank you for that." He motioned toward Bonner's house. "Could I come in?"

The two talked for almost an hour. Olsen explained that he'd heard from his doctors about Bonner's cancer. "I have a check for you, something to help with your medical costs." The man shrugged and gave Bonner a slight smile. "Maybe it'll help you get the care you need."

Then Olsen asked Bonner about God. And, with Angela at his side, Bonner told him about their faith and about living a life right before God. At the end of the conversation, Olsen and Bonner prayed.

"Could you be my friend, Bonner? Someone I could

visit now and then, someone to talk to about God?"

A smile lifted the corners of Bonner's mouth. He squeezed Angela's hand. "Definitely."

"Good." Olsen stood to leave. "I was asking God about a friend when I crashed. And now He's worked everything out." Olsen walked to the door, looked over his shoulder, and grinned. "I think He's going to work everything out for you, too, Bonner."

When the man was gone, Bonner turned to Angela and remembered the check. "He gave me something, a thank-you gift."

"Well, open it up." Angela stood beside him, peering at the folded check.

Bonner did, and both he and Angela fell silent, shocked.

The check was for one million dollars. In the note section it read only, "Use this to get better."

Bonner did just that. In the months that followed he tried the costly experimental treatment. Three years later, in one of their many times together, Bonner and Olsen agreed that God had done more than take part in the miracle of Olsen's rescue and Bonner's healing. He also gave them the miracle of new friendship.

The Wedding

JOHN P. WALKER

Jack and Jean were among our earliest friends when I began ministry in my very first church as a full-time pastor. Their friendly faces and warm smiles were a great encouragement to a young preacher with the Sunday morning pulpit jitters. Their smiles were genuine, which was a surprise to me, as they had been through more trials than almost anyone I had ever known.

Jack had been a chemist with a successful company. Over a period of ten years, a diagnosis of a severe form of rheumatoid arthritis took Jack from a healthy workingman to someone confined to a wheelchair and living on a disability pension. By the time I met him, he could move himself from the wheelchair only with great difficulty, and then, only to shift to another chair, or to stand for a moment. Pain and effort showed in his face when making these transitions, which were usually few and far between.

He and Jean got around well in a new van converted for the wheelchair. A small elevator installed in their townhouse moved Jack between the floors, and in spite of his misshapen, arthritis-bent fingers, Jack learned to use a computer and assisted us at the church with some of our financial work.

Through Jack and Jean, I also came to know their now adult daughters. When Susan, the eldest, arrived at my office to ask me to perform a wedding for her and her fiancé, Eric, it was no great surprise. Her father had hinted only a few weeks earlier that this might be coming.

The counseling and the planning of the ceremony seemed to go by very quickly, and soon it was almost time for the wedding. One day, Susan made an unscheduled stop at my office. From the look on her face, I knew that something was seriously wrong. She came straight to the point. "My dad wants to walk me down the aisle," she said, close to tears. "He really thinks he can do it. He absolutely insists on it."

"I'll practice until the wedding. I'm going to do this," he told me adamantly while sitting at his kitchen table drinking tea the next day. "Please pray for me!" I knew there was no changing his mind when he was determined to do something, and so I let the subject drop. I did, however, pray.

When the evening of the rehearsal arrived, we set up several scenarios that would allow Jack to "present" the bride. Only one of the three involved him walking down the aisle, and we included it only to please Jack.

A brief experiment that evening seemed to deflate Jack's determination as he only took a few steps before he had to sit back down. From the platform, I watched sadly as he hung his head where he sat. Again, I prayed.

The day of the wedding arrived. Everything was going as planned. At the top of the hour, I found myself standing on the steps of the platform with groom and groomsmen, awaiting the bridal party.

The music began playing, and the bridesmaids proceeded down the aisle. Each paused and turned as she passed the front row of pews and took her place opposite the groomsmen. The maid of honor was last to walk, and as she turned in her appointed position, the music softly concluded.

After a brief pause, the organist played the dramatic opening notes of the wedding march. "Will you all please stand," I instructed.

I found myself thinking of Jack. He had been brought up the steps to the sanctuary in the lift earlier and now waited in the wheelchair by the door. With the struggles of the previous evening still in mind, Jack would not be walking the aisle today. I was disappointed for his sake, but I couldn't imagine his hurt. This had meant so much to him.

The doors to the church sanctuary opened to the side at the rear. This meant that the bride would have to walk behind the last row of pews before turning into the center aisle. I could just make out Susan's progress above the heads of the now standing congregation because of the puff of white taffeta that stood up from her veil.

I saw that puff of white stop, and then murmuring began near the back. A moment later, the beautiful bride made her turn into the main aisle. It took a second to realize what was happening. Susan was being escorted by her father, and he was walking!

Slowly, and painfully, Jack took a few steps and then paused to catch his breath. With a cane in his left hand and her arm on his right, father and daughter moved toward me. It seemed as if the entire congregation was holding its collective breath, all of us fearing that the next step would be the last. I believe, in that moment, we were all unified in prayer for Jack.

The organist looked at me with panic in her eyes as the music came close to its conclusion. I motioned for her to continue playing, and a few more minutes inched past before the bride and her father finally arrived at the front.

As the music concluded, I quickly gathered my thoughts. Still awestruck, I voiced a rather shaky introduction. I almost choked up when I asked, "Who presents this woman to be married to this man?"

Jack's voice came back clear and strong, and not without some measure of pride, "Her mother and I do."

As Susan hugged her father and then took her place alongside her soon-to-be husband, I noticed that her face was wet with tears. I noticed my own face was wet! In fact, it seemed like the whole congregation had been as deeply moved.

The wedding reception that followed was a wonderful affair. It was one of the grandest I had ever attended. But, whatever the charm or excitement of the post wedding celebration, the highlight of the day, in everyone's eyes, remained the miracle we had witnessed shortly before. The miracle of Jack, with determination born of love, and faith in the living God, escorting his daughter down the aisle on her wedding day!

No truer words express the miracle of that day as those written in Mark 10:27: "With man this is impossible, but not with God; all things are possible with God."

CHAPTER 2

Facing Our Fears

"Men will faint from terror, apprehensive of what is coming on the world, for the heavenly bodies will be shaken. At that time they will see the Son of Man coming in a cloud with power and great glory" (Luke 21:26–27, NIV).

Of all the crises we may face, the most devastating is fear. For when we are afraid, we let go of our faith and our trust in God and try to live on our own. The result is that we become more weakened and more distant from God. When we are overcome by our fears, we must reach out our hands and hold onto God with all our might. His strength will enable us to stand up again, to confront whatever threatens us, and to move ahead out of darkness into light.

The Moose and a Miracle

KERRY SPRAGUE

I tossed and turned in bed, trying not to wake my husband, Don, who slept peacefully beside me. My heart raced, my palms were sweaty and I could barely breathe. Another panic attack was keeping me awake.

I had struggled with anxiety for nearly twenty years. I had tried everything, counseling, medication, acupuncture, you name it, I tried it and nothing helped. I felt worthless as a wife and mother of two girls. I could barely cope each day; much less take care of my family. I prayed as the tears silently trickled down my cheeks, "Lord, please take my life. I can't do this anymore." I was too afraid to take my own life, so instead I begged God to do it. I wiped my tears away with the edge of my comforter.

As I watched the sun rise and brighten the sky, dread filled me. I had to face another day. My husband knew about my anxiety attacks but he had no idea how I longed for my life to end. No one knew that.

I forced myself to get up. I had two little girls who needed to eat and we were getting ready to go on a two-week road trip to visit the national parks throughout the western United States. Our plan was to start with the nearby Rocky Mountain National Park in Colorado, then visit Wyoming, Montana, Alberta, Idaho, Washington, and back through Wyoming to our home in Boulder, Colorado. I should have felt excited about this vacation but I just feared the trip. As I packed the girls' bags I hoped that two weeks away would give me some relief from my anxiety. Maybe I'll see a moose, I thought as I zipped up the last bag. That might bring some joy in my life. I had seen a moose once when I was a little girl and had always wanted to see another one.

The next morning, after another sleepless night, we loaded up our Jeep and buckled the girls into their car seats. I took my spot in the passenger seat, and tried to put on a smile.

"We're off," Don said. "This is going to be a great trip."

"It'll be fun to be away for a couple of weeks," I said. I didn't want to disappoint Don so I pretended to be excited, but inside I was scared. I worried about the car breaking down, where we would stay at night, if the girls would get sick, if the weather would ruin our trip, if Don would have fun. I fought the panic that threatened to smother me.

I did my best to appear cheerful and enjoy the trip, but I continually battled panic attacks. I also kept secretly wishing to see a moose. This became more and more important to me as we covered more miles. I wanted to see one, to remember the joy I felt as a child, to know I could have some relief from my anxiety, even if for a moment. This would somehow give me assurance that I could be okay in the future. As we neared the end of our vacation my hope to see a moose faded. The usual gloom I felt began clouding my thoughts as the rain clouds darkened the skies. We entered northern Wyoming in a thick fog, making it difficult to see much, but on the side of the road I noticed a moose crossing sign.

"Okay, girls, you know how we haven't seen a single moose on this whole trip?" I said, looking over my shoulder. They nodded their heads in unison "Well, I need you to help me spot one. Can you guys keep your eyes on the lookout for a moose? This is where we might see one before we get home."

The girls, Don, and I began searching the hillsides, trying desperately to see a moose. This game helped pass the time, but no luck—no moose.

On our last day of the trip I had given up all hope of seeing one. I fought back the tears that were pooling in my eyes. It was time to go home and continue fighting my unending battle with anxiety. In desperation I silently cried out to God, Lord, I need to know if I'm going to be okay. Will You please show me a moose?

But, Lord, it can't be any moose just walking out of the woods—it has to be something unique. I need to know it's a sign from You that I'll be all right.

We were only a few hours from home as Don turned into Dubois, a little town in Wyoming, to get gas. As we came around the corner into town I couldn't believe what I was seeing. On my right was a car wash and on the roof of the building stood a giant concrete moose.

"Don, stop! I have to get a picture of that moose," I practically yelled.

"What?" he asked.

"You're not going to believe this, but I just prayed and asked God to show me a moose, a sign from Him to me, but not just a moose off in the distance, but somehow unique, so I would know it was from Him."

"Well, that's definitely unique," he said as he smiled and pulled into the car wash.

I grabbed my camera, stood in front of the beast and clicked. WHIRRRR. "Oh, no, I'm out of film! I have to have a picture of this."

We drove around to a few nearby stores but it was Sunday, after 5:00 PM, and all the stores were closed. Yet I still felt excited that God had answered my prayer. We drove home.

Unfortunately, during the next five days, my anxiety drastically increased. I hardly slept or ate anything. Don asked his mom to come over and help with the girls because I could barely function. I thought often about that moose, but as time went on, and I became worse, my thoughts turned negative. It wasn't a real moose anyway. Or that probably wasn't from God. I chided myself for holding hope in seeing a silly concrete moose.

Then on the fifth night I hit rock bottom as I stared at the static on the TV in our family room. "Lord, please either help me or take my life," I pleaded again. I tried to sleep on the couch, but kept watch as the clock slowly ticked toward morning. Around 3:00 AM I heard a still, small voice say, "Look for the cross in the moose picture."

What moose picture? I didn't get a picture of it. I'm losing my mind, I thought as I rolled onto my back. Then I heard it again, "Look for the cross in the moose picture." I must be making this up. Then I heard the same words for a third time. Maybe I'm not making this up. Okay, I'll take the film in tomorrow.

The next morning, feeling ridiculous about what I was doing, I prayed, "Lord, if that voice was from You last night, then let me grab the right roll of film." I reached into the brown paper bag that held forty rolls of undeveloped film, and grabbed one roll.

I went to the grocery store, dropped off the roll at the one-hour developing counter, and shopped for an hour. When I picked up the film, my hands were shaking. I desperately wanted to see a cross in the picture, but I didn't even know if this was the right roll of film, or if I even got that picture of the moose. I opened the envelope right there and flipped through the pictures.

Then I saw it, the moose on top of the car wash. I had captured it on film after all. I stared at it, looking for a cross. My eyes studied the moose, then the clouds in the sky, and suddenly a shiver went through my body. There in the sky were two jet streams crossing over each other—A cross! "Wow! Thank You, Lord," I whispered.

When I got home I called Don. I told him about the voice I heard in the night and the picture. I choked back sobs as I said, "I can't believe God would do this for me. I know I'm going to be okay."

From that moment on my healing began. For the first time in twenty years I began to see results. I felt purpose in my life. I began doing things I never would have dreamed of doing before, like teaching a Bible study, speaking publicly, and volunteering in my daughter's classrooms. I even slept peacefully, and ate normally. Slowly my anxiety disappeared and was replaced with an excitement for life and a peace that was foreign to me.

I still keep the picture of that moose with the cross in it as a reminder that God healed me from my anxiety. But, more importantly I know God answers prayer. He answered mine in a way that had meaning just for me.

The Power of Prayer

BETTY R. GRAHAM

When my eldest sister, Hazel, married Earl, her childhood sweetheart, they moved to an apartment just a block from our home in Lansdowne, Maryland. Until that time, Hazel had slept with the rest of us girls in the front bedroom of Dad's house. The four of us shared two double beds in that room. As the youngest girl, my place was in the bed with Midge, next to the wall; Hazel and Helen occupied the other double bed. After Hazel left to live in her own apartment, Helen had a bed to herself.

Then World War II began and young men all over the country joined the military to defend our country. Our brother, Bud, joined the Army, along with several of his friends from our town. Earl joined the Navy and was assigned as a pharmacist's mate on his ship. When Earl was shipped overseas, Hazel returned to our house to stay until Earl could come home.

My sisters belonged to a church group called the In-Betweens. It was made up of young and older people who were not in the service—young women whose sweethearts and loved ones had joined the military, and even men and women who were too old to serve in the military. This group decided to write letters and send packages of cookies and goodies and news of the town and church to all those who were serving their country in the time of war. They compiled a newsletter called "The Mail Call Blues," which included up-to-date news of what was happening at home, as well as news and addresses received in letters from the servicemen scattered in all parts of the world.

I was too young to be a member of the In-Betweens, but I felt I was a part of it because the newsletter was prepared in our home with my three sisters working energetically to get it ready to mail to our men in the service. They even gave me the job of going through magazines to cut out cartoons and jokes to paste into shorthand tablets to make the men laugh. We received many letters from the soldiers and sailors who received the newsletter, saying how much they enjoyed it and even requesting that we send it to nonmembers of our church who were serving with our young men.

One night I was awakened by sounds in the next bed. I didn't know what was happening. I sat up and saw my sister Hazel sitting up and praying as hard as she had ever prayed. Tears ran down her cheeks and she told us that she had a terrible feeling that Earl was in danger. The only thing she could do to help was to pray. We all prayed for Earl with her. Finally we were able to go back to sleep. It was more than a week later when Hazel received the news that Earl had been wounded. We were all distressed, but we followed Hazel's example of thanking God that Earl was still alive.

Not until she had received a letter from Earl did Hazel know what had happened. We learned that Earl's ship had been in a terrible battle. A Japanese kamikaze plane had crashed into the ship, killing and wounding many American sailors and leaving a huge hole in the deck where the elevator had been. We had to wait many months until Earl returned to the States to learn the details and, even then, they did not come from Earl. We learned that Earl was to be awarded the Silver Star for his bravery during that battle.

We were told that after the plane crashed into his ship, Earl had raced on deck, bringing wounded men to sick bay for treatment. He made many trips until he himself collapsed. He had not even realized that he had been wounded until he dropped from loss of blood.

Today there is a scar on Earl's neck from that wound. A piece of shrapnel caused it. If it had landed an inch either way, his spinal cord would have been severed and Earl would not be here with us now. When he and Hazel compared notes of the time that the battle had taken place, Hazel determined that it was the exact time she sensed that her husband was in danger. The only thing Hazel felt she could do at the time was to pray.

The only thing?! It was the best thing she could do, the best thing that any of us could do to help. Prayer works miracles.

We're Trying, God

JUDIE GULLEY

It's midnight, and my son is not home yet. Another set of car lights starts down our country road, and my heart pounds with hope. The familiar ache that spreads through me as the car speeds past our driveway is so powerful it takes my breath away. With my arms crossed tightly, I pace in the darkness from the living room window to the front door and back again.

I didn't give him a curfew. He's twenty-two, after all, and a college man. It's not like it was when he was in high school and I had the right to give him orders. Now he has to arrange his own destiny. It's all up to him.

Or so they tell me at Al Anon.

"Let go, let God," they say. I have to quit cleaning up his messes. He's a man now, making a man's choices and decisions. He has to take responsibility for his actions. How else will he learn?

But it's so hard. This is the child of my heart, the baby I held close in my arms. How can I throw him into the cold darkness and turn my back, leaving him to find his own way?

I'm trying, God. Just send him home safely one more time.

Fear less and love more, they tell me. I try not to think about bad things from the past. The speeding tickets. The wrecked cars. Calls from the police. Those who know—who have been through it—tell me to live now and for the future. Don't regret the past.

Easily said. So difficult to do.

The clock's minute hand inches its way past twelve. The fear eats away at me.

I think about the last accident, the last trip through court. How I sat behind him and listened as the attorney read the charges: "Driving under the influence, driving with a suspended license, leaving the scene of an accident..."

This can't be my child he's talking about. Not my son with the bubbling sense of humor and laughter glinting from his marvelous blue eyes. The little boy who hugged me each night at bedtime and said, "I love you, Mom." The tot who giggled with excitement as he wobbled off on his first tricycle. The baby who smiled back at me since the day he was born.

Not my son.

When the hearing was over, he turned to me, his eyes puffy and red and filled with a hopelessness that made me want to hold him and never let go. "I need help," he whispered.

Now, after six months of AA meetings for him—

Al Anon for me—I see signs that give me hope. He's treading cautiously, thinking carefully about each move before he makes it. The old buddies don't call or come around now. He's home most nights, in bed at a decent hour. He does these things without anger, without resentment. I want so badly to believe, to trust. But this is the first night he's been out with a friend, and my old fears are bubbling to the surface.

He's trying, God. Bring him home safely just one more time.

More lights start down the road. I hold my breath until they swing into the driveway. Then my knees tremble with relief. I switch on the light next to a chair in the living room and pretend to be reading. A car door slams. I hear him laughing.

The back door opens. When he sees me, he hesitates, and I see the flash of hurt in his eyes. He wants badly to be trusted. But he's adult enough to know that it's too soon. He sighs and smiles.

I try to smile, too. "I couldn't sleep," I tell him. "I'm sorry."

"It's OK," he says. "We stopped to get some pizza after the movie. I didn't even think about calling."

The same old criticisms rise to my lips and die there. I study his face, thinking what a handsome man he's become, looking for some sign of the baby I held for the first time, twenty-two years ago.

I know I've got to let him go. He knows it, too. He

leans over and gives me a hug. "I love you, Mom," he says softly.

"I love you, too," I whisper back.

I feel the tears curling up into a remote corner of my mind...to sleep...just to sleep. But we've made it through tonight. We'll take tomorrow when it comes.

As he climbs the stairs to his room, I turn out the light.

We're trying, God. Thank You for bringing him home safely one more time.

Finding the Strength
to Overcome

RENIE SZILAK BURGHARDT

When I moved to this beautiful, hilly rural area from a city twenty-two years ago, I was finally realizing a lifelong dream. My children were grown and living lives of their own; it was finally my turn to live a life of my own, surrounded by God's beautiful nature. And I have done just that, roaming these hills and woods at will, enjoying the wildlife, and teaching my grandchildren about them whenever they came to visit from the city. It was a life I loved and hoped to continue for some time.

Then one day this past December my life changed in an instant! We had a light snowfall the day before. Only a couple of inches of snow, but it was enough to make things slippery outside. It was a Saturday, and earlier that day my friend, Jan, and I had an enjoyable time eating lunch at a restaurant, and shopping in a large department store. I got home later than usual, and rushed to feed the animals.

It was very late afternoon when I noticed the bird feeders needed refilling. Cardinals, chickadees, gold and purple finches, and a multiple of other birds were waiting for their supper before they would settle down for another frigid night. And as I walked up a small hill to get to the feeders, carrying a bag of wild bird seed, I suddenly slipped, and landed on my right side with a thud!

Of course, I fully expected to get right back up again, and continue my walk to the feeders. But when I tried to get up, the worst pain I have ever experienced shot through my right side, making me cry out, and I quickly realized that I was not going to get to the feeders or anywhere else, for that matter!

It was already past four in the afternoon; it would be dark in another hour, and I had no close neighbors who might see me and come to my aid. And I didn't have my cell phone with me, as I'm supposed to at all times, to call someone for help. Panic gripped my heart as I also realized that if I was going to spend the night outside, I might freeze to death! Somehow, I had to find a way to get into the house. Still trying to rely on my own strength, I tried to get up again, with the same result: unbearable pain, and no success.

"Dear God, I'm in big trouble here, and I need Your help. Only You can help me now. I pray for Your wisdom and strength. Please help me get back into the house. I trust that You will help and sustain me, but whatever happens now, Thy will be done, Heavenly Father, Thy will be done!"

Tears welled in my eyes as I prayed. Then, closing my eyes, I lay there a while, feeling the chill of the snow-covered earth beneath me, and slowly resigning myself to the inevitable—spending the night outside.

But suddenly, a soft whisper of a suggestion entered my head. "Try to crawl into the house. You will have the strength to do it. I will give you the strength."

"Oh, I don't know if I can, Lord. I don't know if I can."

"You can, if you try. Trust in Me, and try."

When I was a little girl, a long time ago, I believed I heard God's voice. I don't think anyone else believed me, but I knew I did. And now, He was speaking to me again, of that I was certain.

I decided to try and crawl up the hill to my front door. Somehow, I suddenly managed to move slowly toward my destination. There was a lot of pain with every move, but I kept crawling. It took me an hour to get to my front door, but as darkness descended I finally was able to make it into the warm house. Exhausted, I lay on the floor for a few minutes and rested.

Finally, I moved again, reaching the sturdy wooden chair in the dining room and somehow managed to pull myself up, holding onto its back. On the table lay my cell phone. With shaking hands, I reached for it and punched in my son Greg's number.

"I'm hurt. I think I broke my hip. I need help!" I cried into the phone in an anguished voice when he answered. "I'm in so much pain, I can barely stand it." Fifteen minutes later, a sheriff's deputy car and an ambulance pulled into my driveway. Greg, who lives two hundred miles from me, was on his way.

"The door is unlocked," I called out as I heard someone knocking, still standing in the dining room, holding onto the wooden chair with all my might. Within minutes I was in the ambulance, speeding toward the hospital and help. The kind woman attendant even gave me a pain pill, and asked me how and where I fell.

"I was outside, trying to fill the bird feeders, and slipped in the snow," I told her.

"Outside? But how did you manage to get back into the house?" she asked incredulously.

"When I realized I couldn't make it in on my own, I prayed for help. God gave me the strength to make it into the house, " I said, grateful tears rolling down my cheeks. "Sometimes it takes a crisis to make one realize once again that God is always near, and all we have to do is ask for His help. He will never let us down." The woman attendant in the ambulance nodded and stroked my head gently.

And now, just a few months after my accidental fall, as I am still recovering from hip surgery, I thank Him daily for being there whenever I need Him. With his help, I am even able to walk again without the aid of a walker, although a small limp still remains to remind me of what had transpired: a true miracle. But, according to my doctor, the limp will also be gone, soon enough, and I'll be as good as new. And I have Him to thank, for the rest of my days.

You Must Be Brave

CARLA M. ZWAHLEN

Y ou must be brave," said my beautiful husband. You must be brave? He must be kidding. The peril we faced suffocated me. Being brave was about as far removed from me as the life we knew and the future that fast slipped from our grasp. Where would I find brave in the midst of this nightmare?

Werner's oncologist appointment ended and staggered us with the diagnosis: stage III esophageal cancer at the stomach junction, with a few lymph nodes adjacent to the tumor affected. The treatment protocol included months of chemo and radiation therapy, followed by a massive radical esophagectomy, the likes of which I can't begin to comprehend. I wasn't brave, I was numb.

Eighteen years ago, there were other hospital stays, and hours Werner and I spent sitting in the grip of nerve-wracking waiting room chairs. That was when our eight-year-old son, Stefan, underwent neurosurgery to remove a brain tumor. Three years later, Stefan's neurosurgeon removed another brain tumor. Here we were again, hospital bound, for more waiting and wondering, this time for Werner's fight. The long day of doctor consults and tests finally ended. Exhausted, we headed for the exit doors through the busy hospital rotunda. Although I didn't see exit doors ahead, I saw flashbacks of Stefan's fight merge with Werner's battle, just beginning, and my emotions, like the worn seats on those waiting room chairs, slid downward. I lagged behind Werner in order to harness my crumbling mood before I faced him.

I thought my external expression masked my inward turmoil. It didn't. Werner saw through the mask. I looked ahead among the steady stream of people exiting the huge glass doors, and saw Werner step out onto the noisy portico sidewalk. The hum of car engines idling while people helped patients get in and out of vehicles, created quite a din under the high-ceilinged portico. Once I caught up with Werner, we walked only a few paces away from the big doors when Werner stopped abruptly in the middle of the people traffic.

As my private husband, not known for courting public attention, turned to face me, the sheer determination in his eyes jolted me. I didn't know his intent, but his action was surprisingly uncharacteristic. He had my utmost attention. Gently, he placed both of his strong hands on my shoulders, and his brown eyes—along with four words, "You must be brave"—pierced my heart.

Time can stop for seconds. Suddenly people seemed to move past us in slow motion. The car noise slowed and muffled down to the sound of an old phonograph record played at the wrong speed. Inside that time-frozen moment, Werner met the first challenge of the fight for his life: me. He came forward and rescued my courage from a crushing avalanche of fear. The soul of our wedding vows spoken thirty years ago—through sickness and in health...to love and to cherish...until death do us part—also lived in that moment.

Written in his eyes I saw these pleas: Promise me you will be brave. I am forced to attempt the most threatening and difficult climb of my life. You and I are roped together. If you let go of the rope, I cannot fight. I will suffer enough, but my suffering will be unendurable if I must watch you suffer, too. Just as suddenly as he stopped me under the portico, he dropped his hands from my shoulders, turned away from me, and resumed his walk toward the parking lot.

Did I respond to his request? I must have said, "Yes, I will be brave." Of course, I said yes.

I don't know if I said yes or if I said anything. I was dazed. It all happened so suddenly and ended just as quickly that it was dreamlike. Yet his plea to me was powerful and pivotal for the time to come. His courage to face the first challenge of his fight defined the way he wanted to deal with cancer. I shook myself out from the daze, and when I caught up with him, we did not speak. I just felt his fingers wrap themselves around mine.

I drove toward home along a narrow winding mountain road. Darkness covered the road and my thoughts. At least driving prevented the tears, but ominous visions and questions took root in my spirit like uninvited weeds that grew in my garden. Who will help me to be brave in the face of esophageal cancer living in Werner's athletic body? Where is the brave that will hold me strong on the rope with Werner, after months of aggressive toxic chemotherapy drugs and radiation kill Werner's healthy and diseased cells? Where is the hope against the odds of Werner surviving this beast?

Brave, what brave? Brave means I must be fearless and bold. It's more my character to worry. Where is bold in that?

The miles flew by and panic waves built up around me. I held my breath against the black sea of suffering this cancer portends for Werner. I feared I'd soon drown in those thoughts, until somewhere in the whirlwind I heard a quiet voice say, "Look at Jesus."

Tired and battered, I looked at Jesus. The quiet voice spoke again. "Your terror, like Peter's, is a keeping-your-eyes-on-Jesus moment. Do you remember how Peter learned to trust the Lord, when he, along with the other disciples, were at the mercy of a midnight storm on the Sea of Galilee, and were terrified? Then they saw Jesus appear out of the mist like an apparition? When Jesus told Peter to walk to Him out on the water, did Peter say, "I don't trust You to keep me from drowning? What did Peter do?"

"I remember," I said. "Peter fixed his eyes firmly on Jesus, stepped over the boat rails, and against all the laws of physics, stood firm upon the waves."

The quiet voice spoke, "Trust Jesus! Nothing else will work. Keep your eyes on Him. He will keep you from drowning in your own maelstrom. He will show you how to be brave."

Yes, of course, I told myself, God would be my brave. I will trust God.

"Really?" a familiar and mocking voice spoke. "You are going to ask God to be your brave? Why?" Now the mocking voice had my attention.

"Isn't God the one who allowed this cancer's threat upon Werner's life? You should be angry with God. Remember your son's brain tumors. You thought, after the first brain tumor, it wouldn't get worse. Who allowed the second brain tumor to grow?"

"Yes," I said to the mocking voice, "God allowed those awful circumstances, but He also said, 'Do not be afraid or surprised when life hands us trials.' It's you, the adversary, who manipulates misery in the world. You try to make me lose my trust in God. I can't choose my circumstances, but I can choose whose voice I will listen to and whose directions I follow."

The quiet voice spoke again. "Nothing can separate you from God's love."

That's true. God promised never to leave me, no matter what my circumstance, I reminded myself.

Again, the quiet voice spoke, "Keep your eyes on Me, as Peter did when he trusted Me to stand him on the storm waters."

The mocking voice was silent.

I asked myself, "Would my anger against God help Werner's fight?" The answer was clear. If I chose to handle Werner's illness with bitterness and despair, he'd see my discouragement and be forced to expend more energy to fight under my dark cloud. Certainly, my anger would add to his misery.

Yes, I was sad and weary when I turned the car into our driveway, but the despair was gone. God had replaced the fear with the promise of Himself. God chose Peter's lesson to reassure me that, however difficult the forced climb Werner and I must attempt, I can trust Him for the courage I need to honor my husband's request. Keeping my eyes on the Lord, I was ready to begin.

Silent Treatment

KATHY MATTEA

I had never experienced anything quite like it. Late in 1991 I was performing at a club in London. Near the end of the set, I was singing "You're Not the Only One" when I reached for a high F near the top of my vocal range. What came out, however, didn't sound like me. I felt like a rock climber grabbing a familiar handhold only to have it crumble away.

I got through the final number and an encore, but as I walked offstage the band gathered around me. Those guys knew my voice inside out. They could tell it had been more than a simple missed note.

My manager rushed backstage. "Are you all right?" he asked, concern tightening his voice.

"I'm fine. Just a little tired." My mind was racing. All singers have ups and downs. No one is one hundred percent every night. You just learn to sing around problems. My schedule was booked tight, and I had obligations to promoters, audiences, my musicians and crew. To stop would mean more pressure than going on. I couldn't quit. I had been on an award-winning streak for three years, and I had waited all my life for the touring opportunities I now had.

I've loved music ever since I can remember. I was a precocious kid, and early on teachers warned my mom to keep me busy so I wouldn't get bored. She threw me into every activity she could think of, and music was the one thing that stuck. It never bored me; there was always something to learn. I learned piano and guitar, then started singing. Eventually I began playing folk Masses at our tiny Catholic church in Nitro, West Virginia, picking guitar and singing solos. We lived in Protestant country. The Baptist church across the street let out halfway through Mass, and I can remember our priest trying to speak over the steeple bells, which were thirty yards from our open church doors.

We strained to hear him, and tried not to get the giggles at how comical the situation was. There was something earthy and real in our little church. The music was heartfelt, and everyone sang as loud as they could. My years there taught me that music is a way to embrace God, and I never doubted where my singing came from.

After two years at West Virginia University, studying engineering and physics, I missed music so much I decided to move to Nashville. I had always dreamed of a music career, and I prayed for guidance. I didn't care if I became famous; I was in search of a more interesting life. After some rough months, I began a spiritual ritual of putting myself in God's hands every day. I prayed for a path, a niche, and I prayed for clear vision. If I didn't have what it took, I wanted to be able to let go and get on with my life.

But I found my path, and it had led to the stage in London that night. Exciting things were happening, yet they were coming at me so quickly I didn't have time to enjoy them. I started feeling the pressure of success, the double-edged sword that it can be. Some mornings I woke up more tired than when I went to bed. When I began to question my feelings, the guilt kicked in. Who was I to complain? How many people would like to be exactly where I was now? Didn't I have everything I ever wanted? Hadn't God put me on my path? I began to wonder if I was having a nervous breakdown.

After the London show I flew back to Nashville. At that point I couldn't even sing. The next morning I saw Dr. Ed Stone at the Vanderbilt Voice Clinic.

"Just relax, Kathy," he said as he passed a fiber-optic instrument attached to a video camera to the back of my throat. I tried to breathe and stay calm. I looked at a monitor. The camera would show my vocal cords, a pair of membranes no thicker than a nickel that produce a miraculous range of sound.

"Say, 'Aah.'"

"Aah. . . . "

I saw my epiglottis move and then something truly horrifying. I expected my cords to be raw and red, even a bit swollen, par for the course after a long run. But I had never seen anything like that—a large red ball, like a blood blister, directly on top of one of the cords. Instinctively, I pulled back and gasped. Before I could stop myself, I was sobbing.

Doctor Stone let me cry for a while, then softly encouraged me to let him take a closer look. I wiped my tears and tried to compose myself. "Kathy, you need complete vocal rest," he said. "You must not sing. You must not speak, not a word, not even a whisper. Try not to laugh. You need to rest. Not just your voice but your whole body. Take a little time off. Relax."

After three weeks, the doctors at the Voice Clinic would have another look. We would learn more about our options when they could see my cords without the swelling and inflammation. No one said it, but we were all thinking surgery. I had three weeks of nothing to do but worry about the future.

My manager had come to the clinic, and we discussed canceling all my engagements for two months. He didn't blink an eye. "Done," he said. I drove home and explained the situation to my husband, Jon. That was the last I would talk for twenty-one days.

It was strange taking time off in the middle of summer, usually my heaviest touring season. And it was odder still to be utterly silent. No rehearsals, no meetings, no interviews, no chats with friends. I went from ninety miles an hour to a screeching halt. At first it was uncomfortable, and then I began to feel peaceful. I listened more. I began to realize how much I used my voice to define myself, in all aspects of my life. And I had no choice but to sit quietly, alone with myself even in a crowded room.

That day, after my conversation with Jon, I laced on an old pair of running shoes and hit the beautiful walking trails of Radnor Lake, a nature preserve six miles from downtown Nashville. I needed to take some action in order to feel I was contributing to the healing process, and that was my first step.

I started going for long walks every day. As I wandered through the sun-dappled woods on the ridge overlooking the lake, I held silent conversations with myself and listened for answers. At first, the walking gave me comfort—the feeling of getting away from my problems. But as time went on, my physical exercise became spiritual exercise. I thought about my priorities. I thought about the role my work played in my life. I worked hard, and I loved it. Still, I felt overwhelmed by success, and at times my life seemed out of control. Where had I gone wrong?

I thought back to simpler times in my life—to West Virginia and our little church. I had found my voice there. It had felt so right to sing. Had I ruined my voice by doing what I thought God wanted me to do? How could I make sense of that? What if I couldn't sing ever again? What if I was never the same? Waves of fear would wash over me, and I'd cry uncontrollably.

But during my walks I began to face fear and regard it as my constant companion. I would visualize it as a small creature that lived on my right shoulder. It looked, in my mind, like a gargoyle. It wasn't going to go away, but I had God on my side. Eventually I became bold enough to talk to it. In my mind I would say, I can't get rid of you, but I am going through this to the other side, and God is going to lead me. I began to realize that I had no idea what God had planned for me. Maybe there was some other path I was supposed to take, and this was His way of getting me there.

I began to see small signs. While waiting for a CAT scan of my neck to check for tumors, I spotted a little girl, about five. She was on her dad's lap, and I could see a catheter tube peeking out from under her gown. I looked around the room at an elderly man on a gurney, waiting as I was. He was pale and thin. And I realized that those people had much bigger struggles than I had. My condition was not life-threatening. I would go on, voice or not. I would find the next thing to do. Suddenly I knew it would be okay, that God was indeed taking care of me, in His own way.

As my daily walks continued, I began to realize it was my soul as much as my body that needed healing. I began to see my injury (my "ruby," as I had come to nickname it) as a gift. Nothing else would have gotten my attention in the same way.

I surrendered myself completely. And I was truly ready for whatever happened next.

The three weeks of silence passed quickly, and after another three weeks of vocal therapy, I cautiously returned to singing. I began to tour again, and even recorded another album. I was living with the injury and doing well, until it hemorrhaged about a year later. Surgery became unavoidable at that point. It was a bit of a roller-coaster ride, but I had new reserves and my physical and spiritual rituals to get me through it. I just kept turning everything over to God. He was in control—not me, not my fear, and not even my doctors, ultimately.

The surgery was a success and today my voice is stronger than ever. More importantly, my faith is stronger. Like my body, it needs daily exercise. When I do my spiritual calisthenics life doesn't seem so complicated and stressful. Everything certainly does not always happen the way I want it to. I have setbacks and disappointments. I question as much as I accept. But that's how I grow.

Earlier this year I went through some soul-searching.

And for one of the few times in my life I asked God for a concrete answer. I sent up a prayer asking for some confirmation that I was offering something with my singing. I said, "If I'm supposed to quit, just let me know. I'll go on to the next thing if it's time…"

That night, while I met fans after the show, a woman was walking away after having her picture taken with me. She stopped, turned around, took hold of my arm, looked me directly in the eye and said, "Don't quit. Your music means so much to us."

It was all I needed to hear.

The Healing

PAT MEHAFFEY

You had a dream, only a dream. Don't panic!"
"But every detail appeared crystal-clear. The sounds, the smells, the colors."

That conversation went around and around in my mind at four o'clock one morning after a powerful nightmare awakened me.

My mother died in a nursing home after several years as an Alzheimer's patient. She died twenty years ago, but I continue to feel a strong aversion to entering any place filled with the sick and elderly. To me, such a place epitomizes total hopelessness. Through force of will, I had recently progressed to visiting the residents in the lobby, but I still could not step inside the individual rooms. My nightmare changed all that.

In my dream, I served as a volunteer in a hospice facility and a nurse summoned me to the room of a frail, wraithlike woman whose breath of life could continue for only a few hours. All color and expression had drained from her face and hands, and her thin body scarcely lifted the bed covers.

Noticing her dry, cracked lips as I entered the room, I quickly and carefully moistened them, smoothed her hair from her forehead, and took her weightless hand in both of mine. She appeared immersed in an ever-deepening coma, drifting irretrievably away from mortal existence. My heart swelled with tenderness and compassion, and an urgency to pray and recite scriptures filled my mind. I had begun quoting the Beatitudes when the nurse came and stood beside me.

"She can't hear you," she said.

"We can't be sure of that," I replied, and then with bowed head, I recited Psalm 23. As the beautiful words, "Yea, though I walk through the valley of the shadow of death," echoed through the room, I opened my eyes and looked at her calm face, seeing a glow that now shone around her. Her breath came regularly but softly, and an accepting look of serenity showed plainly upon her face.

Her breaths became farther apart as I continued to hold her hand and stroke her face. In a voice filled with certainty, I reminded her that God loved and cherished her as His own child.

At last the shallow breathing ceased and the life-light faded away. After a long and difficult span, her aged, non-functioning body received the ultimate healing. The Holy Spirit filled my heart and mind with the assurance that she did not die alone. Perhaps my presence at the point of death offered final comfort and affirmation of her life.

Yes, I had a dream. Of course, I did.

For over twenty years just the thought of an elderly person approaching death always gave me a panic attack. Repeatedly, I fled from the room, out into the fresh air, rather than share any contact with those nearing the end of their earthly journey. Consumed with cowardice, I couldn't even minister to those nursing home residents who needed their hair combed or their nails trimmed. I simply could not force myself to touch them.

But in my dream, my thoughts and actions seemed so real—so right—and my behavior felt satisfying and obedient. Did this dream reveal a sign from God showing me that my emotions had recovered from the effects of the dehumanizing illness that destroyed my mother? Could the dream convince me that through Him, I have the fortitude to stand at the bedside of the dying and make a difference? Has the wound on my soul healed?

The dream occurred two months ago and I've wasted no time. With confidence and peace since that night, I frequently visit residents in our local nursing homes. Sometimes I just hold their hands and sing softly. Occasionally, I read scriptures of comfort and assurance. I have conversations with those patients who are alert and responsive, and I come away with new knowledge and blessings.

Contacting an area hospice, I learned they offer training for people who want to assist in the final care of terminally ill patients. A need exists for me to share my strength, my respect, my Christian love and my certain knowledge that God cares for the dying.

Through my own healing, I received power to minister to others. My dream presents absolute proof that all believers "can do everything through him who gives me strength" (Philippians 4:13, NIV).

The Gift of Dance

KAREN KINGSBURY

Isabelle Sims had never felt more discouraged in her life. She was twenty-five years old with a noticeable weakness on her left side, the effects of being born with cerebral palsy. And that afternoon she had attempted the impossible. She had joined more than seventy applicants for the position as dance instructor at a prestigious New York arts school.

Part of the interview had included a solo dance routine. Isabelle had the credentials and experience, but there was no way her dance held up to those of the other young women—women who were free from the handicap she'd lived with since she was born.

She left the building in tears and made the hour-long ride to her mother's house in the country. *She'll be so disappointed.* Isabelle thought of how badly she wanted the job, how it'd been the single dream she'd nurtured since she was a young girl. Dance instructor. Helping other children find the wings to fly across the stage the way she would have done if not for her handicap.

The moment her mother answered the door,

Isabelle's heart broke. Tears filled her eyes and she fell into her mother's arms.

"Honey, what happened?" Isabelle's mother, Lucy, held her tight, finally helping her inside where they sat in the living room side by side.

"They'll never hire me." Isabelle covered her face with her hands. "The other applicants were graceful and smooth. Who wants a dance instructor who can't walk without limping?"

Lucy looked gently at Isabelle for a moment. Then without saying a word she stood, searched through her video cabinet, and slipped a tape into the VCR. When she returned to her spot next to Isabelle, she hit the play button.

The screen came alive with the image of Isabelle as a beautiful nine-year-old, twirling and leaping in the air, her ballet costume floating gracefully about her knees.

"My first dance recital." Isabelle stared at the image of herself and wondered how she'd lost touch with that young girl, the girl she'd once been. "I had so much confidence back then."

Her mother stopped the film and reached for Isabelle's hand. "You were such a little fighter back then, sweetheart. Nothing was going to stop you. Especially not a bothersome case of cerebral palsy."

Isabelle sniffed. "That was a long time ago." She

ran her fingertips beneath her eyes and shook her head. "That little girl doesn't exist anymore."

Lucy drew a slow breath. A sad smile lifted the corners of her mouth. "Darling, I think you need to hear the miracle story one more time."

Isabelle shrugged. She'd heard the story of her birth a dozen times, and it always brought her comfort. Hope. Maybe her mother was right. She sat back in the sofa and focused her attention on her mother. "Tell me."

Lucy's smile grew. Isabelle could see in her eyes that she was drifting back in time, back to a day when no one thought Isabelle would survive the first year of her life. Back to a time when doctors thought she'd never walk, let alone dance.

"It was 1984," Lucy began, "and I was expecting a child. Pregnancy had never been easy for me. Especially after Charlie and Chase."

Tears moistened Lucy's eyes as she reminded Isabelle of her small sisters who had died before they were big enough to be born. The miscarriages meant that when Isabelle's mother got pregnant with her, the doctor was very concerned.

"Your father told me that since the boys had been fine, there was every reason to believe God would grant us a healthy baby, even after the miscarriages." Lucy's chin quivered. "But I was worried anyway. I wanted you so badly, Isabelle."

At the time, the Sims had lived twenty minutes north of Beloit, Wisconsin, and Isabelle's mother planned to deliver her without pain medication. As long as she could carry the baby to term, the doctor did not expect any problems.

"I prayed daily that you would survive the pregnancy and that God would give me the wisdom and peace to cope if problems developed."

Lucy drew a deep breath and continued the story. As the pregnancy progressed, she had developed a constant low backache. But she told herself this was normal, since most pregnant women had back pain. One morning, though, when she was twenty-four weeks pregnant, she had been at work when she realized she was having regular muscle contractions across her abdomen.

"False labor," I told myself. "Don't worry about it."

But when the contractions continued throughout the morning, steadily increasing in intensity, Isabelle's mother telephoned the doctor.

"'Sounds like a false alarm,' he told me. 'Rest a bit and they should stop.'"

Instead the pains got worse. This time the doctor told her to go straight to the hospital. An hour later tests confirmed that Lucy was indeed in labor.

"They told me you couldn't survive if you were born then." Quiet tears ran down Lucy's cheeks.

"While the nurses set up an IV with drugs to try and stop the contractions, your father took my hand and prayed out loud with me. We prayed for a miracle."

Isabelle imagined how her mother must have felt. "Were you scared?"

"No. I was sad at the thought of losing you, but I wasn't scared. I knew God would do what was best. And even though no one else believed, I knew in my heart you were going to live."

Isabelle's mother continued the story: minutes had become hours and Isabelle's father had fallen asleep. About that time the medication took effect and Lucy's heart began to race.

"Suddenly I couldn't draw a breath. I tried to stay calm, but when I opened my mouth to yell I couldn't force out enough air to make a sound. Finally I found the nurse's button. While I waited for help, I pinched off the intravenous line to the medication. About that time your father woke up and realized the crisis. He shouted for someone to come quick."

Lucy shuddered at the memory. "Nurses came immediately and realized I was having a rare side effect to the medication."

One of the nurses had placed an oxygen mask over Lucy's face and ordered her to breathe. In ten minutes the danger had passed for Isabelle's mother.

But not for Isabelle.

"Without the medication, my labor pains grew worse. An hour later they flew me to Chicago where the hospital would be better equipped to deal with that type of extreme premature birth."

A technician had performed an initial examination and checked Lucy's labor. Afterward, a neonatologist met with her and did an ultrasound. On the screen appeared a small body, perfectly formed. It appeared to be a girl, wiggling and even swallowing.

"I fell in love with you then and there." Isabelle's mother wiped at a tear. "I begged God to let you live. 'Let me have my precious little girl.'"

Two days later, despite the doctor's efforts, Isabelle was born. Doctors were clear in their warning: at that stage of gestation, there was a strong chance the baby might die at birth. Isabelle was too fragile to undergo a regular birth and had to be delivered by C-section.

"I was awake through the whole thing. I wanted to see you." Lucy's voice broke. "Even if it was only for a few minutes. I did nothing but pray throughout the operation."

Twenty minutes after the surgery began, Isabelle Suzanne Sims was born. She was fourteen inches long and she wiggled furiously, trying to draw her first breath.

"The doctor took one look at you and said, 'She's a fighter.'" Lucy uttered a sound that was part laugh, part sob. "After that I believed that somehow you'd survive. It was almost like watching a miracle take place before my eyes."

Isabelle's heart swelled with love as she pictured her mother, staring at her in those early moments and praying for a miracle. She felt her present disappointment ease as her mother resumed the story.

"Even though you were long for such a young baby, you weighed just over one pound. The doctors were very worried. They immediately sent you to the neonatal intensive care unit and put you on a ventilator inside a small, sterile covered bassinette. Your skin was so translucent, we could see the capillaries underneath. You were red!"

Three days later, when Lucy was released from the hospital, Isabelle was still gaining ground.

"I knew you were gong to make it," Lucy grinned through her tears. "God had made it clear that He had special plans for you."

For the next three months, Isabelle had grown and gained ground in the hospital. A brief sponge bath in her bassinette and the holding of her tiny hand was all the contact Lucy was allowed for weeks on end.

"You would kick at the wires and tubing around you." There was a distance in Lucy's eyes as she saw again the image of Isabelle at that age. "I was so proud of you. 'Keep fighting, Isabelle, baby. Keep fighting.'

That's what I told you every day we were together."

Isabelle and her mother had been surrounded by death during those three months. Because of its skilled staff, the hospital typically had sixty premature babies in its care at any given time. And one of those died every day while Isabelle struggled to survive.

"They wrapped you in plastic wrap until your own skin began to grow. It was truly amazing to see you survive a little more each day."

Finally, after four weeks, Lucy got to hold her daughter for the first time.

"It was the most emotional five minutes of my life." Fresh tears filled Lucy's eyes. "To have you in my arms, where you belonged. I couldn't do anything but thank God for the miracle of your life. You were working so hard, too, to fight off infections and life-threatening illnesses. Everyone I knew was praying for you."

Isabelle felt cushioned in the blanket of love that had welcomed her into the world. She locked eyes with her mother and listened.

When Isabelle's weight had climbed to five pounds, the doctors gave her permission to go home. At that point her body systems were also functioning on their own—a necessity before a premature baby can leave the hospital.

"The doctors told us the risks were far from over." Lucy's voice grew softer. "Cerebral palsy was the primary concern. When a baby is premature, even a slight jarring motion can cause the brain to bleed. When that happens, cerebral palsy is the result."

In Isabelle's case, a sonogram had detected a low-grade bleed during her time in the hospital, so the Sims knew to look for cerebral palsy. Once she was home, a physical therapist monitored her condition weekly.

The months passed and became years. Until she was two, Isabelle had numerous incidents where she stopped breathing—a common condition with premature babies. But each time she was able to start again on her own.

"Each time your father and I would thank God for saving you. And each time we reminded ourselves that you were a fighter. You wanted to live; and that was the greatest part of the miracle."

When Isabelle was a toddler, it had become obvious that she struggled with her gross motor skills.

"The doctors told us that though it was a miracle you were alive, you definitely had cerebral palsy on your left side." Lucy began to cry and put her hand over her mouth. Isabelle reached for her hand, tears stinging her own eyes. After a moment, Lucy found her voice once more. "The doctor said you would never learn to walk."

Isabelle's parents had talked over the diagnosis and decided that only God could determine whether

Isabelle would ever walk. After all, He'd brought her this far. Certainly He'd see her through to whatever plans He had for her life.

As Isabelle grew, she encountered numerous challenges. But with every obstacle, she fought to overcome. She and her brothers developed a close friendship and never did her cerebral palsy keep her from playing with them.

Suddenly Isabelle remembered something Lucy used to tell her when she was little. "Remember what you used to say?" she said, squeezing her mother's hand. "You'd tell me I was special, and that cerebral palsy wasn't a restriction or a problem. It was a reminder of how blessed I was to be alive."

"Yes." Lucy wiped her tears from her cheeks. "You learned to walk by the time you were three and when you turned six, you began to dance."

At that point in the story Lucy hit the play button on the remote control and again the image of Isabelle as a young dancing girl lit up the television screen.

Isabelle could hardly see the picture through the tears in her eyes. I wasn't supposed to walk, she thought. Yet there I was, dancing across the stage. Dancing. And no one in the world could have made me stop.

When the segment ended, Lucy leaned over and hugged Isabelle close. Then she tenderly touched a single finger to the area over her daughter's heart. "The fighter is still in there, honey. No matter what happens with the job, keep fighting. Because all of life is a dance."

Isabelle clung to her mother's words while she waited for word about the position. During that time, God worked in her heart as she hadn't allowed Him to work in years. No longer was she discouraged by her limitations. Rather, she was reminded that every day, every breath, every step in the dance was a reason to celebrate.

And that attitude made it all the better two weeks later when she received a phone call from the art school.

"Isabelle," the caller said, "we'd be honored if you'd accept our offer of a position at the school. We think you'll make an outstanding dance instructor."

It was the very best dream come true. Isabelle imagined how her mother would take the news, the way it would prove her right again that Isabelle was a living miracle. In that moment, Isabelle knew without a doubt that her mother was right about something else, too. The music still played; indeed, it would always play.

And never again would Isabelle stop dancing.

Painting Life by Numbers

KATHRYN LAY

Numbers are important. I've learned telephone numbers, birthdates, social security numbers, drivers' licenses and fax numbers. I praise my daughter for learning her numbers and how to use them. A whole book of the Bible is dedicated to numbers. But it wasn't until recently that I fully realized the impact of numbers in my life.

After two years of not feeling well, of praying for more energy, my doctor and I began the search for a cause. I would wake up in the middle of the night with a racing heart, a feeling that I was going to pass out and never wake up again. Sometimes these spells came during the day, suddenly and terrifying.

First came the blood pressure and pulse numbers to watch. Then came the cholesterol and triglyceride counts. As a result, fat content numbers and percentages were read, counted, and calculated.

Then came the new numbers that detailed the level of my blood sugar. Results...high.

Declaration... "Mrs. Lay, you are a diabetic."

Now I have new numbers to add to my cast of many. I left the doctor's office afraid, confused, and frustrated that my life had just become more complicated, that the necessary act of eating and planning meals was becoming a career. I questioned God and prayed that the doctor was wrong.

But more tests showed that the doctor hadn't been wrong. I looked at my four-year-old daughter and cried. Would I live to see her children?

Numbers again. A daily sugar count and the grams of sugar in my food must come before taste or familiarity. Grocery shopping became a lesson in mathematics. My once-quick excursions to the store quickly changed into lengthy reading sessions. I considered taking a lawnchair along.

After a while, I became fairly adept at looking at the number of grams and counting, adding, dividing, then moaning or rejoicing.

On my first trip to buy groceries after learning of my diabetes, I was shocked and frustrated at the sugar content of the food and drinks I had previously enjoyed. The majority of what I picked up was returned to the counter.

Too much fat.

Too much sugar.

Too much of both.

I became angry at the thought of the food, full of

these culprits of bad health, waiting on the shelves for unsuspecting customers. Then I became frustrated. Again I questioned God's plan for my life, wondering how taking medication and checking my blood sugar every day would fit into my busy lifestyle.

Wasn't there anything I could just enjoy, I shouted at a bottle of catsup? Anything? Something that wouldn't cause guilt, fear, or affect my health?

Then I saw it. A can of sardines. I used to love them when I was a kid. I shook my head. There had to be something wrong with them, too. I turned over the can and stared in wondrous surprise at the low fat and sugar content.

Like a girl on her wedding day, staring at her new husband, my emotions took hold. I clutched the sardines and cried. It was something I liked, and I could eat it. I glanced around to make sure no one was watching my display.

As the first year has passed, I've found my attitude changing. I've met and read of others with adult-onset diabetes. I've found that it is life-changing, yet not life-disturbing, unless allowed to become that way.

Friends have asked what has kept me motivated to continue walking, to stay on my diet, to lose the weight, to go on with my normal activities. I tell them: fear of complications and wanting to feel better. But, I know it's much more.

It's the joy in my young daughter's eyes as we play ball in the backyard or laugh together at the amusement park. It's the times of friendship, intimacy, and planning for the future with my husband. It's the conversations and good times we have with our friends. It's the satisfaction and fulfillment of seeing my writing published and of speaking to school kids.

People who've dealt with cancer or other diseases struggle to understand that they are still loved and have a place in life. I've talked with some who say that others look at them differently when they know. Then they see themselves as little more than a vessel for their illness.

Yet God has given me so much more.

I am a diabetic. My mother is a diabetic and her mother before her as well.

But, even more, I am a wife, mother, daughter, sister, friend, writer, neighbor, speaker, Sunday school teacher, club president, teacher to my daughter, companion to my husband.

Although I carry my diabetes with me, it's only a small part of who I am. It took months to accept this, to understand that I have a full life ahead of me, the same as the day before my doctor's announcement.

I learned this from my four-year-old daughter. "Sweetheart, Mommy is...well, kinda sick," I explained one day when she asked why I stuck my finger every morning.

I went into a long, yet diluted explanation of my diabetes, that I couldn't eat things with sugar and that I had special medicine to take.

She listened patiently, then said, "I'm sorry." After a moment, she took my hand. "Mommy?"

"Yes?" I asked.

"But can you still play with me?"

I grabbed her in my arms and said, "You bet!"

And life has gone on. And I number every blessing it brings.

CHAPTER 3

The Comfort of Memories

Great is my boldness of speech toward you, great is my glorying of you: I am filled with comfort, I am exceeding joyful in all our tribulation (II Corinthians 7:4, KJV).

Looking back over the losses of those we have loved can be heartbreaking. But the memories can also make it possible for us to hold onto the love we have known. Letters, photographs, words we remember, times we spent together, do not end. They stay with us forever. That's one of God's many blessings.

The Messenger

LONNIE HULL DUPONT

I was very close to my mother, and I was fortunate to have her until she was eighty-four. In the end, cancer took her, but she always planned to beat it. Although she had confidence in where she would be in the next life, my mother really and truly did not want to leave this one, and she fought hard to stay here.

In the last six weeks of my mother's life, with the help of Hospice she stayed at my sister's house a few country miles from my own house. During this time, Mom and I spent lots of time together, talking. I wrote in my diary then: "It's a sad time but a soft time." I knew she was dying, but she never seemed to accept it. Once she told me, "I sleep so well at night now. Then I wake up thinking of all the things I'm going to do, and I'm ready to jump up and do them." She seemed bewildered as she looked down at her cancer-riddled body. "And every morning, I'm so surprised that I can't."

Two days before Mom died, I dreamed I was standing in a cemetery next to my car. Two young men, both wearing dark suits and dark glasses, approached me. I felt nervous about them, so I hurried into the car and hit the lock button. They watched the locks snap down. I cracked my window, and one of them said, "Will you tell us where you're going?" I refused, and I raised the window back up. Then I turned the car around and drove away. I watched them in the rear view mirror to see if they would follow, but they simply watched me drive away. When I woke up, I felt that God had sent me a message to prepare, that my mother's passing would be soon.

The next day was very difficult for Mom. Overnight she had lost the ability to speak clearly. She could express herself with her eyes, gestures, and head nods or shakes, but her speech was garbled. She badly wanted to talk, and it seemed she had something important to say to us. But try as she might, she could not say it.

Finally at one point, my mother gave up trying to talk and began to keen. I do not come from a culture of people who keen, and it was a frightening sound to me. When Mom eventually quieted down, she curled into a fetal position and went into a deep sleep.

Mom was still breathing when my husband, Joe, and I drove to our house early that evening. We were drained from this emotionally difficult day, so we didn't talk much. We simply went to our bedroom and tuned in television news, prepared to turn in early. Our two cats joined us on the bed.

We lived in a large old farmhouse, and our bedroom was what had once been a front parlor. It was next to the central hallway and front door, so when I looked out the window on my side of the bed, I could see the side of the front portico of the house.

It was almost dusk. The news blared away. I was aware of the cats running over me at some point to get to the open window on my side of the bed, and I could hear a bird, but thought nothing of it. The huge yew bushes outside the windows had lots of bird life, and that brought plenty of viewing thrills to our housecats.

Joe muted the TV and said, "Listen." The cats sat at the window, their tails slapping hard on the bedside table. There was a loud, insistent chirp coming in from the screen. I saw to my surprise one red cardinal on the yew branches, looking at the window screen, chirping hard.

I grew up in the country and of course knew some birds. But my mother really was more attuned to them. She taught me to watch for the first robin of spring, which after a long Michigan winter was wonderful to see. My mother kept bird feeders and wren houses, and she fed birds in the snow when she still wintered in Michigan. She often told me that she hated to see a bird in a cage. "They should be outdoors and flying, not caged up," she would say.

So I knew a little about birds, and while I didn't recognize the chirp of this bird, I certainly could recognize the scarlet brilliance of a male cardinal. He was so close and so loud that the cats were simply beside themselves.

Neither Joe nor I had any idea why this bird sat vocalizing fearlessly into our open window as dusk approached. He hopped from yew branch to the portico and back again, over and over, his chirping loud and insistent. One of the cats made her signature "kill" noise—a fast clicking of her back teeth—but even that didn't unnerve the cardinal. Our talking didn't, either.

"Do you think his mate is hurt or something?" I said.

"Let's see," Joe said. We stepped outside, and the cardinal moved to the top of the portico. He did not fly away, and he did not stop chirping. We investigated the porch and surrounding grass, even under the yews, but we saw no reason for this cardinal to be so agitated. So we went indoors.

The bird moved back to the yews and window, and he continued chirping. He chirped so loud that when a friend called on the phone, I finally shut the window so I could hear her better. He chirped outside the closed window for awhile longer and eventually flew away. As I fell asleep that night, it occurred to me that, like the men in the dream, perhaps the cardinal might be some kind of messenger, but I fell asleep while trying to figure it out.

At 5:00 AM, my sister called to say we'd better

come. Mom passed a few minutes before we arrived. But seeing her body at rest made us all realize how free from pain and frustration she was now. My family and I sat next to Mom's bed for a time. Her room had an east window, and as the sun was rising, my brother-in-law remarked, "Look—a cardinal." Sure enough, a bright red cardinal swooped by the window. I briefly told my sister and brother-in-law about the chirping cardinal of the night before, but we all had other things on our minds right then.

That sad day lumbered on. Hospice came, the hearse came, relatives came. We made arrangements, we picked out clothes for our mother, and then Joe and I drove home. Now it was Sunday afternoon, still the same day my mother left us. Exhausted, Joe and I crawled into bed for naps. The cats joined us as the wind picked up outside. A storm was brewing in the southwest.

But I could not sleep. I began to feel panicky. I had never been in this world without my mother. She and I talked to each other almost every day of my life, and now I could never again even call her on the phone. I gave up on the nap and got up.

I walked through the house, looked out the windows, and cried. It slowly dawned on me that in all this activity of Mom's illness and death, I hadn't noticed that spring had come and gone. We were already on the cusp of summer. Seven huge maple trees, each four stories high, stood guard around the west and north sides of the farmhouse, and they were fully leafed out. Now their branches and leaves moved wildly in the warm wind.

I figured there was still time before the storm would hit, so I moved to the patio where I could cry without waking Joe, and I sank into a wicker chair. The sky in the west was deep gray and turbulent. The maple leaves moving in the wind were getting noisier by the minute, and those high branches creaked. Birds had apparently taken cover. I listened and watched, and I cried. It seemed that nature was expressing my feelings.

And then I heard it. Over the sound of the trees in the wind was a loud chirping. I looked up, and there in those majestic maples was a male cardinal. He swooped from tree to tree, in and out of the green branches. He was the only bird out there that I could see or hear, and he was noisy and bright red against all that green. In spite of the approaching storm, he seemed to be doing what he was born to do. It's not just that he seemed fearless; he was having an absolute blast, as if this were his own personal playground. I watched him soar and swoop and dance around in the heavy air of this approaching storm. I listened to him chirp over the sound of the wind. For the first time in days, I felt my stomach unknot.

I suddenly knew that somehow, some way, this was from my mother. It had been so the night before, it had been so this morning, and it was now. Somehow, some way, I was being brought comfort, and it was coming from her. I felt assured right down to my toes that my mother was free of the virtual cage of aging and illness that kept her from moving and talking. I also knew without a doubt that she was not lost to me forever, that I would join her some day.

How long did I sit there? I'm not sure. But while I watched that flying, dancing, noisy, beautiful bird, I stopped crying.

The next morning, I rose early and went to my computer to write the eulogy for Mom's funeral. While I sat at the keyboard, I heard the chirping. I looked out my window, and there on the south lawn—a lawn with no trees—the red cardinal stood in the grass, as vocal as ever. He was framed in the only window in the room. I felt comforted and went back to my writing.

For the next couple of days, the cardinal hung around the house, mostly in the yews. It began to feel natural to see this little guy. I actually sat next to an open window once and talked to him, and he stayed right there, perched on a yew branch, cocking his head at me, chirping. I began to believe that when we die, some of us don't leave this physical world right away. I felt my mother was still hovering, half in, half out.

As the week went on, however, the cardinal moved farther and farther away. No longer did he sit on the yews next to the window. Sometimes I could hear him but not see him. I had the sense that my mother was moving farther away, more fully into the next life.

Then I had a vivid dream.

In the dream, my mother called on the phone from the next life to assure me. Her voice sounded young and happy, and I could hear her smile as she talked. I started crying, and I told her how much I missed her. She cooed in her motherly way. She told me that she was the cardinal. "I wasn't sure if I should be a yellow bird or a red one, but I decided to go with red," she said, and that sounded so much like her.

The day before, I had covered her grave with red rose petals, and I told her about it in the dream. She said she knew, and she raved at how beautiful the roses were. I asked her what she was trying to say to us on that last day when she could not talk, but she gently indicated that I could not ask about her time with us.

She had an almost secretive happiness, like someone who is engaged or pregnant but not telling anyone yet. I said, "You're not quite gone away, are you?" She said that was true, but she was almost gone. She gave me a phone number I could try at a certain time to reach her, though she couldn't guarantee she'd be there. I started to feel panic because I was losing her smiling voice. Then the connection broke up. I hung up and tried the number, and it would not work. Then I woke up.

That was one week to the day since Mom had died. My friend, Jeanette, came over for Sunday dinner. After we ate, Joe left us alone, and Jeanette and I took our iced teas to the patio. It was a stunning day, and the birds were vocal in the maples. I decided to take the risk and tell my friend about the cardinal.

Jeanette was very moved, and she agreed that the bird was a messenger of some kind. Then I told her my dream of the night before. This was the first I'd talked about it, and when I finished, Jeanette said, "Listen...."

Up in the trees was the bold chirping of one cardinal, louder than all the other bird sounds. Jeanette and I looked at each other, then we tried to find him. We followed his chirp all around the seven maples in the yard, and although we both heard him loud and clear, neither of us was able to catch sight of him. The next day I no longer heard him. The cardinal seemed to have left. I believed my mother's departure from the physical world was now complete.

The year anniversary of my mother's death came on a Monday. I dreaded its arrival, but it turned out that I would be hosting a meeting in my house all that day. I was grateful people would be around. I woke up that morning to a steady, gentle rain that would last all day.

Joe and I had left the farmhouse a few months before and moved to a small house in the next county. No more towering maples, but we did have apple trees and willow trees in the yard and lots of windows. My guests remarked on the windows, and we had our meeting.

Something so sweet happened that day that I asked the others to verify what I saw. In the backyard, then the front yard, then the backyard again, back and forth, a flock of cardinals, both male and female, played in the light rain. All day. On the first anniversary of my mother's death, I was not alone in any way. God sent me perfect comfort.

A Gift of Love

MARGARET CHEASEBRO

J ane Nelms awoke the morning of August 29, 1975, at her parents' house in Denver, Colorado, with labor pains.

"It's time," she told her mother.

She knew what her mother must be thinking. She could hear the words echo in her mind to the same percussion of pain and guilt she had felt since she married Chad. "You should not have gotten married, and this baby is a big mistake."

Jane's mother didn't like Chad or the fact that he had moved out of the young couple's apartment when Jane was six months pregnant. And she didn't think Jane was ready, at age nineteen, to be having a child.

After Chad left, the company that employed Jane went out of business. She had no choice but to return to her parents' home. She knew she had failed her family by making poor choices. They loved her, but she didn't think she deserved their love—or God's. Not she, who had been rejected by her husband. She was unworthy.

After the labor pains began, Jane called Chad at the gas station where he worked.

"Please come to the hospital with me," she begged him.

"It's your baby," he said. "I don't care what happens to it."

Over and over, she pleaded with him to come. He refused. By the time Jane arrived at the hospital with her mother and sister, she was an emotional wreck. She was embarrassed to be there without a supportive husband. She felt like a failure, worthless, facing a future that looked as bleak as a barren plain.

After Jane was wheeled to the labor room, two nurses appeared. One of them was heavy-set, middle-aged, average height, with a calm, soothing voice. Her name tag identified her as Mary. She looked motherly and huggable, and her presence made Jane feel safe.

Mary soon dismissed the other nurse by saying, "I can handle things from here."

Standing beside Jane in a white uniform, her dark hair a contrast to her light complexion, Mary asked, "Have you taken birthing classes?"

"No," Jane replied, thinking that was one more thing she had failed to do.

Mary taught Jane how to breathe so she could deal with the pain. Jane loved her calm voice, so different from the raised voices often used by her family.

By 4:00 PM, Jane's labor pains had intensified. About that time, Chad arrived with his parents, who had forced him to come.

Mary had to tend to her other patients, but she popped in frequently to check Jane's pulse and blood pressure. When the nursing shift changed later that evening, Mary didn't go home. She stayed to be with Jane.

By 11:00 PM, Jane was fully dilated, so she went to the delivery room. Chad went, too. He stood on Jane's left side, and Mary stood to her right. She explained everything that was happening. She tried to get Jane to push. But things weren't going well. The baby's heartbeat began to weaken. Someone gave Jane an epidural. It made her sick, and she threw up. She needed oxygen, but she fought the oxygen mask, afraid she would throw up again and choke. Finally, Mary leaned close to Jane's face and said in her soothing voice, "You need to do this. The baby needs it." Mary's voice helped Jane calm down enough to accept the mask.

"Your baby is fine," Mary kept reassuring her. "You just need to keep breathing."

Mary didn't seem to care about the circumstances that had brought Jane to this place. She wasn't concerned about whether or not Jane had made a wise decision to marry and get pregnant right away. Her focus was on Jane and how she was doing. Mary continued to assure Jane that she would be all right.

"They don't think there's enough room for the baby to come," she explained later. "The doctors are trying to decide if they should take you up to surgery." Mary told Jane that a doctor had been contacted who could perform a cesarean section. Her calming voice helped Jane to relax.

When they wheeled Jane into the operating room, Chad was not allowed to go with her. But Mary never left her side.

Michelle was born at 1:30 AM on August 30.

After the other nurses had cleaned Michelle up, Mary asked Jane, "Do you want to see your baby girl?"

Jane looked into her daughter's eyes and examined her perfect features. "She's beautiful," Jane whispered. After spending some time with her new daughter, she handed the baby back to Mary and drifted off to sleep.

When Jane awoke in the recovery room, Mary was gone. Jane was in the hospital five more days, but she never saw Mary again.

After she recovered enough to return to her parents' house, Jane wrote thank-you notes to everyone who had helped her. She addressed Mary's thank-you note to Aurora Community Hospital, thinking it would be delivered to Mary. But several days later, it came back with a note that no such person was at that address.

Jane telephoned the hospital's maternity ward. "A nurse named Mary helped me through a difficult labor," she explained. "I would like to thank her."

"No one by that name works here," the nurse said.

"But occasionally we do hire temporary workers. Perhaps she was just a temp."

After Jane got off the phone, she thought more about Mary. Could she have been an angel? Impossible, Jane thought. She had fallen too far from God, made too many bad choices. God couldn't love her enough to send an angel. There had to be some other explanation.

But the more she thought about it, the more Jane realized that she had truly been given a gift when Michelle was born: a gift of love and forgiveness, and the presence of a kind soul who walked with her through a troubled, frightening time in her life. Mary didn't judge Jane. She didn't criticize her. She didn't remind her of the mistakes she'd made or the distance she had put between herself and God. All she cared about was helping Jane and assuring her that she and her baby would be fine.

If God had orchestrated all of that, Jane decided, then He really did love her. He didn't judge her. He didn't blame her for making poor decisions. He didn't care about any of that—He just cared about her. He cared enough to remind her that she was worthy of love, that she had not been abandoned. And He showed her all those things through the angelic presence of a nurse named Mary.

A Few Perfect Shells

ROBERTA S. ROGERS

That blustery July morning I scuffed along the beach on Topsail Island in North Carolina, where I was vacationing, and thought about the news I'd just received. My father had been diagnosed with inoperable cancer.

An unusually rough tide had washed hundreds of small stones and pieces of broken shells onto the shore. The shells reminded me of the broken relationship I had had with Dad, who was eighty-four. Now I was faced with not only losing him, but also losing the hope that someday we would reconcile, that I would finally gain the unconditional love of this complex and distant man.

I closed my eyes and prayed. God, I need you. And so does Dad. We need your comfort.

The stiff sea breeze whipped my hair. As I finished my prayer, I looked down at the jagged-edged shells underfoot. I felt startled, as if there were a message for me in them, something I was intended to see. I bent down and scooped up a handful. They were hard to hold, sharp and cutting like the painful memories of my childhood. I threw them down. Suddenly a wave foamed across the beach, sweeping away the shells and depositing new ones.

Studying a stretch of sand, I saw here and there a few small, perfect shells. I picked them up carefully, looking at them, turning them over. Could it be that if I looked closely enough at my own life, I would find a few perfect memories of my relationship with Dad?

I stood for a moment, the hot sun on my back, the waves lapping at my ankles, feeling the moist sand harden beneath my feet. Help me, Lord, to find those moments and to let the others go.

Over the next few days as I walked the beach, I slowly began to discover in my heart and to see in my mind's eye those precious and untarnished memories. In the early fifties, after Dad's business failed, he had started a career as a frozen-food broker, traveling New England and trying to interest merchants in this new concept. Sometimes he would take me along when he went "calling on the trade," and I remembered how important I felt, a little girl getting a glimpse into the adult world of business.

I recalled overnighting on the Mohawk Trail and how he, my brother, and I got up with the sun and walked on a misty country road. Dad showed us flowers and told us their names. And once, when I was eight, I fell into a deep depression. It was the only time

I remembered Dad opening up to me. He told me about his own fears and how he tried to believe that God was there to help. Dad's halting faith, so uncharacteristic of him to speak of, helped me find God and fight my way out of depression.

Yes, I had some perfect shells. I would keep them, and let the others go.

In August I went to Connecticut from my home in Maryland to say good-bye. It was not a very private or satisfying moment. Shortly afterward Dad began to deteriorate rapidly and entered a hospice. Yet he held on tenaciously, long beyond the doctor's estimate.

If only I could see him one more time, I thought, back home in Maryland. But my mother and brother tried to dissuade me. "You don't want to see him like this," Mom said, trying to protect me. "I know he wants you to remember him as he was."

Finally, the cancer left Dad in a coma so deep he needed no painkillers. One of the nurses said that she had never seen anyone survive so long in his condition. Everyone agreed that he was holding on for some reason.

I traveled to Connecticut again, this time on a cold Thursday in November. At the hospice I went into his room and sat in a chair next to him, just the two of us, and listened to his hard, irregular breathing. His wasted form seemed to be shrunken into the bed, and for a second I thought, "Oh no; I'm too late." Then I reached under the covers and ran my hand lightly down his bony arm. I found a place near his thumb that was still warm, still soft, still alive. As I held on I began to speak aloud. I told Dad everything I had been thinking since that day on the beach. I said that God was there for him, just as he had told me when I was a frightened eight-year-old.

Instantly, and with absolute certainty, I knew Dad heard me. The tremors that ran down his arm showed me he understood. A healing force flowed between us, peaceful and forgiving and holy.

A short while later my brother entered the room and stood silently on the opposite side of the bed, hunting for Dad's other hand under the flannel sheet. The thought suddenly came to me, "Let's say the Lord's Prayer." I fought the idea, knowing that praying together was not something we did in our family, but the urge foamed through my spirit like a wave. My brother had told me that he felt he could sometimes sense Dad's thoughts, even when he slipped into the coma. Now he whispered to Dad, "You want to say The Lord's Prayer." It wasn't a question.

We prayed as a family, two of us aloud and one silently. Then I leaned over, kissed Dad's brow and said, "I love you."

The next day, with Mom at his bedside, Dad died.

The hospice nurse said he was at peace. And Mom said to me, "He was waiting for you."

Seven months passed and I returned to Connecticut to stay with Mom while she recovered from cataract surgery. In a quiet moment I related my experience on the beach at Topsail Island. Then Mom told me something I had never known: "Whenever we went to the beach," she said, "your dad had the habit of picking up a few perfect shells. He always did that. In fact, I still have some."

I followed Mom into the family room. She turned from the large window ledge where Dad grew his winter flowers and pressed into my hand four perfect scallop shells.

More Than a Thousand Words

DONNA LOWICH

W alter, whatever happened to those pictures I had taken of Jeffrey and Kenny before I had my surgery?" I don't know why I asked, or what made me think of them. The thought hit me out of the blue. More than two years had passed since I had last thought about those pictures.

Walter looked at me, trying to think of just which pictures I was asking about.

"You know, the ones I took with the boys sitting in front of the fireplace."

He shook his head, and said, "Gee, I don't know. With everything going on, I forgot about them. Too bad, they're long lost by now."

"I know," I pouted. "But those pictures would have been so cute, and they would be such a great reminder of the way things were...." The part of the sentence that I didn't say was: "and a great way to keep focused on my therapy so everything can be like that again."

The pictures were taken on the last visit my sister made before my scheduled spinal cord surgery. She brought along my nephew, Kenny, who was not quite three. He and my son, Jeff, who was four, played together all day. Then I sat them in front of the fireplace. The pictures were going to be Christmas gifts for my sister and my mom.

It was November 1985 and only two weeks before my scheduled surgery to repair a herniated disk in my neck. I was supposed to be out of work for six weeks, and then return to life as usual. That sounded like a good plan to me. But there was one flaw:

After the surgery, I awoke in the recovery room, paralyzed from the shoulders down. I was in the hospital for those six weeks and then in the rehab hospital for another five months, returning home on June 13, 1986. My return home didn't mark the end of my work but, rather, just the start of it. I worked every day after that to recover from my paralysis. Between raising my family, and returning to work while continuing physical therapy, I lost track of those photos taken of Jeff and Kenny sitting in front of the fireplace in their new Christmas sweaters.

Now that I remembered the pictures, however, they were on my mind. I thought about calling the pharmacy, but dismissed that idea because it would have been too embarrassing to ask for pictures dropped off for processing so long ago. Instead, I imagined what the pictures looked like, and whether I centered them (I always have a hard time centering), and I played the tape over and over again in my mind of that last visit before my world went topsy-turvy.

"That's it," I decided to myself, "I want those pictures because they symbolize my life the way it used to be and the way I want it to be. Dear God, those pictures would be so wonderful to have...." It was this unspoken prayer that I thought had gone unanswered.

After awhile, the pictures came to mind less and less often, replaced by everyday life and everyday worries. Life was an emotional roller coaster. For every upbeat day when I saw even a little bit of improvement, there always seemed to be a "down" day that emphasized what I still needed to improve. It was with that up-and-down state of mind that I faced the challenge of my physical therapy sessions five days a week.

Then one night, in October 1988, the phone rang after dinner. I answered:

"Hello, may I please speak with Donna?"

"Speaking."

"Donna, this is Tina from Warrenville Pharmacy. I have an envelope of pictures here for you."

I could hardly believe what I was hearing; there must be some mistake. I answered, "I'm sorry but I haven't dropped off any pictures to be developed, at least, not recently."

"These are from a while ago...," she said. She laughed a little. "We're cleaning our files here and I found the envelope."

Stunned, it took me a minute to speak again. "My pictures? You have my pictures? Thank you so much! I've been hoping and praying for a phone call like this. Thank you so much! We'll be down—tonight—to pick them up!"

Walter drove down to pick up the pictures. Coming home, he smiled and said as he opened the envelope for me, "Wait until you see them. You took some great shots of the kids together."

I looked at each picture carefully, trying to memorize each small detail. I picked out one that was especially cute, with Jeffrey and Kenny, their arms wrapped around each other's shoulders, their faces slightly touching. I had copies made for my sister and my mother, so they received their Christmas gifts, albeit after a three-year delay.

I framed my copy, too, and placed it on the shelf in the living room where it continued to give me the incentive to continue my battle to recover the function I had lost. Worth far more than a thousand words, these pictures encouraged me to focus on my physical therapy and to achieve well beyond the dire predictions made by my doctors in the hospital. With the boys grinning down at me, I received the needed incentive to repeat my floor exercises over and over again. I progressed from wheelchair to canes.

Grateful for my pictures, it took me a little time to realize that my prayers had been answered after all; it was just not on my timeframe, but on God's. My faith that God is at work in our lives everyday was not only restored, it was illuminated. The return of my pictures was a relatively small victory in itself. But more than that, it was a sure sign that God was there with me, and it gave me great comfort. With this knowledge, I embraced my physical therapy with a renewed sense of purpose.

Miracles come in all sizes; this miracle, which may not seem significant in and of itself, was a huge, life-changing event for my family and me.

The delay in getting my pictures, as with recovery from spinal cord surgery, was God's way of teaching me that there is no such thing as instant gratification. All these years later, I am still looking forward to the day when I can walk unassisted, and my hands will function more normally. Yet I know now that there is always prayer and hope, patience and hard work. Most of all, I know there is God's loving guidance and help.

The Pitch

JIM McELHATTON

In the summer of '93, my little brother, Pete, and I played a forty-nine game series of Wiffle ball, a baseball-like game played with a yellow plastic bat and a white plastic ball. The forty-ninth and final game fell on the Sunday before Labor Day and came down to the bottom of the ninth. Bases were jammed. Two outs, full count. And one pitch. That's all I needed. From there on out, forever, it would be referred to as "The Pitch."

The kid was up (he was ten then; I was nineteen). If he hit it, he would win. It was late afternoon, and the sky was turning red. The yapping of Jersey Shore seagulls sounded like fifty thousand hollering fans at a sold-out game. I needed one more strike. Just one.

I breathed deep, then reeled back and brought the ball so far down that my knuckles scraped the cement. Specks of blood trailed after the ball. It looked to me like it was thrown with such fury it was actually on fire. Maybe it would even melt before crossing the plate. I knew that I had just thrown the most perfect pitch ever thrown, and that there was no way Pete could connect with it. So I closed my eyes.

I waited for that sweet puff of air when the Wiffle bat whiffs, followed by the thump of Pete flopping on the ground from swinging so hard but hitting nothing.

But then I heard a hard plastic crack.

Contact. Unbelievable.

Just when I thought it was over, that my kid brother had won not only the game, but bragging rights for as long as we lived, I heard something else.

It was a little dink of a sound. The hard grounder had just nicked a tiny pebble on the ground in front of me.

I told Pete later that the pebble had been divinely placed to deflect the game-winning grounder up the middle just far enough so that I could leap and extend my index finger to barely pierce one of the holes in the Wiffle ball and technically catch it—an automatic out in backyard rules because it didn't get past the pitcher.

Ball in hand, I dove on the ground and banged my head on the cement. Through the blood and the tears I saw Pete's face, that poor, sad ten-year-old face.

What joy! I won!

I shared this story again at a recent family reunion, as I always like to do. Sure, I embellished a little here or there, but it's always fun to relive that magical day. Everyone around me smiled as I told the story. But Pete was out-and-out laughing. I can still hear his laugh.

Finally he said, "Well, that's not quite how I remember it, you big doof."

He said I just got lucky. But I told Pete, in front of the whole family, that I didn't care. "I really don't," I said. "Because that pitch, that one pitch, that hit, and that catch—that was the best moment of my life."

Pete looked down and laughed in that "aw, shucks" kid-brother way, socked me in the arm, and said, "Thanks, buddy."

That I told that story, that I told Pete he was the reason for the best day of my life so soon before his life ended, so soon before the worst moment of my life, still amazes me.

It happened on the side of a winding country road in Dennis Township, New Jersey, at 1:30 AM on October 22, 2000. Pete's car flipped a guardrail and went into Lake Dennisville for no reason I will ever be able to figure, although I will forever torture myself trying. Every day, every minute, I think about Pete and about how it's not fair and why, why, why, why?

I was thinking about him and feeling angry and confused about his death on a day when the rest of the world was feeling much the same way. I was inside St. Bernard's Church in Manhattan the day after the World Trade Center fell.

I had gone to New York City because I'm a newspaper reporter in Atlantic City, New Jersey. But I didn't know what to write that day. There were no words for what had happened. And even though there were three thousand people missing under the rubble up the road, I could not stop thinking about Pete. I figured I should just go home. So I left the church and walked around the corner onto Horatio Street. In tears, I headed for the ferry.

Just as I turned the corner, a baseball rolled up and hit the bottom of a tall metal fence in front of where I was walking. There was a playground I hadn't noticed just behind the fence.

In the midst of sirens, smoke, and dust on September 12, 2001, as trucks hauling bodies rumbled past, I saw two kids playing ball.

They were brothers. Matt, thirteen, and William, nine, told me they didn't know what else to do that day. There was no school. And they did not want to stay inside and think. Playing baseball seemed like a good American thing to do. So that's what they were doing.

I talked to them and wrote up a story about them playing ball, scrawling on napkins in a restaurant because I had lost my notebook. I called the story in from a pay phone. It felt good to take my mind off sadness and destruction for a while and focus on a happy story about two boys playing ball. I could almost feel my brother's presence there with me.

As I rode the ferry back home to the Jersey side of the Hudson, I looked up, smiled, and said a silent word of thanks. I knew then that even though Pete was gone, he would remain forever in memories—and in my heart.

Suffer the Little Children

LENORA HITE

The funeral was over, and all the guests and family had gone home. The children were in bed and I sat in the living room, missing my wonderful husband, Mitchell. For more than fifty years we had been together and now he was gone. How would I manage now that the children and I were alone? I believe in miracles, but at that point I couldn't see how we would make it without Mitchell. Our house is in the woods outside of Manassas, Virginia, with no neighbors close by, and I don't drive. As I sat there alone, I thought back to the years I'd shared with Mitchell.

The Lord blessed us with four miracle children. Not everyone I meet seems to feel the way we did about our children. All four of them are microcephalic retarded children. The chance of this happening four times in one family is almost nonexistent.

Fifty years ago we were living in West Virginia and waiting for our first child to be born. I was only twenty-two years old, but I was so happy. We had waited three years for a baby, and at last it was going to happen.

But when Elizabeth was born she weighed only a little over five pounds and she didn't seem to like to eat, so she kept losing weight. When it was time for me to go home from the hospital, I couldn't take Elizabeth with me. She was down to only two pounds. I was so worried about her.

In the next weeks, she didn't improve much and I couldn't sleep. Every time I would lie down and start to doze off, I could see my little baby girl lying in a casket. And I'd be wide awake again. One night I got up and looked out the window and started to talk to God. "Lord," I said. "there's something wrong with my baby. I know it! Please take care of her. We've waited so long for her and I love her so much. Please don't let anything happen to her."

Just then I felt an arm go around my shoulder, and the sweetest voice I have ever heard in my life said, "Lie down and go back to sleep. Your baby's going to be all right."

It was 2:00 AM, and even though I knew Mitchell had to get up early to work on the farm, I woke him and told him what had happened. He didn't try to tell me I was only dreaming. He just said, "Well, then, do what the voice said; lie down and go back to sleep." I did, and I slept peacefully the rest of the night, without one dream.

When you work on a farm, you get up before the

chickens, so Mitchell was up ahead of me. He didn't tell me, but he called the hospital as soon as he got up, and the nurse told him that the baby had passed the crisis at 2:00 AM. She was going to live! We marveled that this good news came at the exact time that I had asked the Lord to save her. There is no doubt whose arm was around my shoulder that night or whose voice calmed my fears. Elizabeth was our first miracle.

We were able to bring her home a few days later. She was such a dear baby. I called her my little "sweetie pie." As she grew, she tried to say those words, but could only manage, "Mommy's seepy pie." She's fifty years old now and she still can't say it.

Elizabeth was about eight months old when we learned that she was retarded, with what the doctors called microcephaly. We didn't know much about this condition, but it didn't matter to us. We loved our daughter, and it just didn't seem to be all that important. We did ask the doctor if there was a chance that any other children we might have could be the same, and he replied emphatically, "No, it's medically impossible for more than one microcephalic child to be born in the same family."

I should have known not to depend on what one doctor said, especially when Elizabeth was two years old, and he said I should put her in an institution and forget I ever had her. "What?" I cried, indignant.

"There's no way in this world this child is ever going in an institution, let alone being forgotten. We love her." Besides, I had always been taught by my parents and in Sunday school that the Lord knows best, and there's a reason for everything, even when we don't understand. Maybe someday we'll understand His reasoning, but for now, it's okay; we feel we've been blessed.

We have never been sorry to have our family, even though all four of our children are diagnosed as microcephalic retarded children. Elizabeth is fifty, Raymond is forty-seven, Charles is forty-four, and Marsha is thirty-nine. Most microcephalic children live only a few short years, so you see why I know mine are miracles. They all are children—they will always be children, but they are special to us and, we believe, to the Lord, too.

Through the years, we have learned some things about microcephalic children. Microcephaly is not a disease. It is a neurological disorder in which the skull is smaller than normal and fails to grow, so these children do not have a large enough space for their brain to grow normally, which is not something that can be corrected, and they are often retarded. It is not hereditary. Microcephaly occurs usually about once in several million births, so that first doctor wasn't deliberately trying to deceive us. In the early days we were told that the average life span of most of these children is no more than a few short years, and that usually they lie as helpless as newborns all their short lives, but modern technology has made it possible to treat the victims so that they can live longer and even function in some ways. Since these children are always highly susceptible to disease, there have sometimes been deaths when one of them contracts a childhood disease such as mumps.

Our children love each other and anyone they meet. We encourage their individual interests and let them express their special likes in their own ways. Elizabeth, an Elvis Presley fan, has about fifty pictures of Elvis on her bedroom wall.

We are all sports fans, rooting always for the Yankees. Marsha took a special liking to Derek Jeter and has pictures and a large poster of that ball player on her wall. She is a good cook and helps with the cooking every day. Raymond is an outer space fan. We all are interested in and watch the televised shuttle launches. Charles is a big help with the garden. Both the boys mow grass not only for our family, but for others as well. And all four of them can embroider, crochet, and knit, making items of clothing for their stuffed animals and dolls, learned from just watching me and others do this work. But they cannot read or write or do arithmetic. Nevertheless we are grateful that our children have learned to live an almost normal life, even though they will forever be children.

We have been fortunate since we moved to Manassas, Virginia, to have the help of very good, caring physicians. The first pediatrician, Dr. Alvin Connor, took a special interest in our family and treated them through the years. He called our children his modern-day miracles. They loved him and felt at ease when we took them to the doctor's office. Dr. Connor is now retired, but his associate, Dr. Arthur Gower, still treats my family, even though they are physically adults, with that same loving care that Dr. Connor practiced. If one of the children needs to be seen by a doctor specializing in adult illnesses, I will take that one to a different doctor, but Dr. Gower treats them for all routine checkups and normal illnesses. I thank God every day for sending us wonderful doctors who care about us and with whom my children can feel comfortable.

But not everyone treats them with such kindness, especially children, who can sometimes be cruel, calling them names and making fun of them. Once, about fifteen years ago, when my husband's job as a security guard kept him away from home for night shifts, I became uneasy. We had heard strange noises outside our house during the night. It sounded like someone was trying to get in. I was afraid that if they did break in they might harm the children. It was then that I began to feel inadequate. How could I possibly protect these beautiful charges of mine. What would become of them if something happened to me or my husband? Who would take care of them? My fears took control of me.

The next day I wouldn't let the children go out in the yard alone. Instead I took them out in the garage and asked them to wait for me while I went to the bathroom. I was only away from them for a few minutes, but when I returned they were all excited, pointing up at the sky and waving.

"What's the matter? What are you waving at?" I asked.

They all answered, "Jesus!"

I questioned them a lot, and they told me that Jesus had come down on a cloud that didn't touch the ground, and off to one side were three crosses and on the other side, an angel. They said that He smiled and spoke to them, telling them that He loved them and not to worry because He was watching out for them and would never let anything or anyone harm them. They described Him as having long, brown hair and blue eyes, and He carried a "big stick." The shepherd's crook, I thought.

I didn't see a thing, but all four of them chattered away excitedly, telling the same story. I would have given anything to see what they saw, but I guess it wasn't for me to see. In that instant my fears disappeared. I remembered the arm that had gone around my shoulders so many years before when Elizabeth was a baby, and I knew that I and all my children were loved. We are not alone.

The memories of all those years calmed my fears. Mitchell is with God now, but God is with us, too. I know He will watch over us all the rest of our lives. And when the time comes for me to join Mitchell, I know that God will show the way. He will provide the right person to love and care for our children as Mitchell and I have done for all of their lives. We have already felt that love from members of our family. I know it will continue.

I have been blessed with our miracle family. I can't think what my life would have been without them. We may never have asked for children like these when we were starting our family, but the good Lord always knows what's best for all of us. I thank Him every day for my four miracle children.

The Car Ride

BETTY R. GRAHAM

I grew up as the youngest in a family of six children in a house on the main road of our small town on the outskirts of Baltimore, Maryland. I was five years younger than my closest sibling, my brother Bob, and twelve years younger than my oldest sister. Bob considered me a brat, probably because until I came along, he had been the youngest in the family.

Bob was a feisty teenager, sixteen, and smaller than most of his peers, but he made up for it by being better in sports than most of them. There wasn't anything that Bob didn't think he could do, and usually, he was right—quarterback on the sandlot football team, scoring many a touchdown because of his great speed and the ability to dodge players on the other teams. When he ran, his knees came up high, almost to his chin. He also could brush off injuries with a shrug of his shoulders. I remember that time and again he'd have a band-aid on his nose after a game. The other teams' players always targeted him whenever he carried the ball, so when he was tackled, there were always four or five players on top of him. But that didn't discourage him. He would hop up, wipe his nose, and get right back to the huddle. He wasn't afraid of anything or anyone, and there was nothing he didn't think he could do. These character traits earned him a lot of friends, but two special ones.

Many days after school, Bob would go out with his two best friends. One of those boys had an old car, but Bob didn't. In our house, there was only one car, a Dodge sedan, which Dad drove to work every day. It was the first new car that Dad had ever bought. No one in the family was allowed to drive that car because Dad said he couldn't take the chance of having it damaged or losing it in an accident and then not being able to get to work. He told us we could learn to drive when we were working and could buy our own car. Bob thought that was unfair, but Dad stuck to his decision. No one else in the family had been allowed.

Mom felt a little sorry for Bob, since most of his friends could drive, so she let him go out with them after school. When the boys pulled up to the front of our house and honked the horn, Bob raced down the steps and hopped in the front seat with the other two. Since he was the smallest, his seat was in the middle between the boys. This happened time and time again. They would cruise around the neighborhood, with no particular destination, returning in about an hour to drop Bob off. He felt he could live with that.

Then one afternoon, the boys pulled up and blew the horn. Bob raced down the stairs to join them, when Mom said, "You can't go today, Bob."

"I can't go. But why?" Bob said, incredulous. Never before had Mom told him he had to stay home. He had not done anything to merit punishment, there was nothing she wanted him to do, and Mom gave him no explanation, but she would not relent on her decision. Finally, the two boys drove off without my brother. He was furious and went upstairs to his room to sulk. He stayed there alone until suppertime.

At the supper table, my other brother, Bud, gave us the latest news. There had been an accident in town. Bob's friend's car was involved.

"Was anyone hurt?" my mother asked.

"No," answered Bud. "The boys were lucky. Lucky you weren't with them, Bob."

Bob's face turned pale. After supper, he asked if he could go to his friend's house to hear about the accident.

"All right," said Mom, "but be home by ten o'clock."

Bob promised and raced out the back door. When he returned much earlier than 10:00 PM, he was quiet, subdued. He had seen the damaged car, but he didn't want to talk about it.

In those days, there was a metal piece that divided the windshield in half. Most of the cars of the day had that feature. And the front seat was solid, running the width of the car, no bucket seats. It made it easy for three people to fit on the front seat, but the person in the middle didn't have as good a view as the other two.

Bud explained why Bob was so quiet. In the accident, the windshield had been broken, and the metal piece was pushed all the way to the back of the front seat—right where Bob would have been sitting if he had been with his friends.

We never learned why Mom had forbidden Bob to accompany his friends on that day. It's possible that even she didn't know why she refused to let Bob go. But there was no doubt that he had been spared by a force greater than all of us, a miracle Mom called it. From that time on, Bob didn't question Mom's decisions.

Unmeasurable Miracle

ANN J. BRADY

I can honestly say that I have witnessed a miracle. I saw a sixteen-year-old boy say, "I love you, Mom." He lifted his wasted fingers up to his tracheotomy, placed one of them over the opening, and spoke the words to his mother. He hadn't been able to speak for four weeks, or to breathe on his own. The ventilator connected to his trach was his tie to living—a thin, threadlike connection to life.

The journey that brought Andy to this miracle began with a broken leg. Inexplicably, while climbing out of the pool after water polo practice, he turned and his left femur cracked. It was a spontaneous fracture—the kind that occurs in the aged, not in a sixteen-year-old. Not unless the bone is laced with cancer.

Osteosarcoma took his leg, all the way to the hip. And a misdiagnosis, or missed diagnosis, started him on this treacherous path. As Andy recovered from the amputation of his leg, his body scan revealed massive lung involvement. Tumors the size of apples and oranges were growing in all the lobes of his lungs.

As a nurse working in the recovery room, I looked up from my work one day to see Andy's name on our list. His was a familiar name, but I didn't really know him. I just knew he was a friend of my sons through their Boy Scout troop.

Scouting didn't fall into my parental job description; it was on my husband's list. Backpacking was for men and boys, or at least I was happy to see it that way. My connection was through chauffeuring duties, through the stories told after the latest camp-out, which sometimes included mention of Andy. But now this boy was on my turf, our orbits intersecting in a manner that I would not wish on anyone.

Andy had been a plucky, boys-will-be-boys kind of kid, as eager to go backpacking and exploring as he was to play a prank on his fellow Scouts. Yet the face I saw when he came to the hospital was masked with pain, fear, and a comprehension of his own mortality that a kid his age shouldn't have had.

He had already lost a leg. Now his only choice, and it was something he had to make a choice about, was a ventilator, massive chemotherapy, and hope. So he nodded yes to the ventilator and gave over control. He lost his voice and gave up weeks of cognition. He chose to fight, to strap on this burden as if it were a heavy backpack. He chose not to give up on hope.

When we read of miracles in the Bible, or hear stories

of them, they seem to be quick flashes of change. The blind man can suddenly see. The crippled man can walk for the first time. In this case, the miracle built slowly, constructed by the prayers and good wishes of many. One of the tenets of Scouting is a profession of belief in God. Our troop represents a cross-section of beliefs: Jewish, Episcopalian, Catholic, and Methodist, as well as fallen-away believers of a variety of faiths. All of them prayed for Andy.

Neighbors rallied. Someone with a connection to a missionary in Africa had a tribe of people praying for this boy so far away. Teachers and students visited and wished him well. The UCLA basketball team crowded into his room and urged him to keep fighting. And, added to the mix of murmured prayers, were those of the teenagers. At an age of uncertainty regarding their beliefs, these boys plaintively whispered in their hearts, Please fix Andy, while they simultaneously shook their fists toward Heaven and cried, "Who are You that You can do this to one of us?" And all these people, from the faith-filled to the dubious, told others about Andy, creating a ripple of good will as palpable as an electric current.

The doctors hoped the chemotherapy would, literally, give Andy some breathing room. The first X ray after the first round of chemo showed a remarkable reduction in the tumors: they had shrunk to the size of apricots. After the next round of chemo, one lung was completely clear, and the doctors began to talk of a "measured miracle." Slowly, Andy's strength began to return. He was weaned from the ventilator and given a fond farewell by the ICU nurses when he left for the regular pediatric unit. Andy's family has even started making plans for him to go home.

There is still a lot of healing to be done. More chemo, plus the constant vigilance of protecting Andy from infection. He'll also have to deal with the painful psychological aspects of the loss of his leg, the loss of time, and the agony of facing a permanently altered future. These are all issues waiting for him—but it's better than the alternative. The plan now is for Andy to finish the chemo, then be fitted for a prosthetic leg so he can walk away from this nightmare.

It makes me wonder that the doctors will only call this a "measured" miracle. Somehow they're more comfortable giving a scientific-sounding twist to what so many of us are convinced is miraculous, plain and simple. Once Andy spoke—and told his mom, "I love you"—there was never a doubt in my mind that the miracle I had witnessed was immeasurable.

The Sign of the Rose

KRISTYNA SZAJOWSKA*

She was such a beautiful baby, an adorable little girl, a joy for our happy family. We were proud of all four of our children, and especially Carol.

That's why it was so hard for me to understand what happened when Carol reached teen age. Almost overnight she became a different person, moody and irritable, a stranger to her father and me. Her whole personality changed, as if some demon had taken possession of our little girl. She would flare up for seemingly no reason, her anger erupting in cutting remarks and foul language hurled at her brother and sisters. She started to take an interest in boys, one in particular who, in our opinion, was much too old for her. But we could control that; we wouldn't let her date without our approval, and we made sure she was at home and in bed at a decent hour. She turned hostile toward me.

It unnerved me, but I attributed it to her age. Although she looked more mature, she was just fourteen. I supposed she would grow out of it. At least she was doing well in school, so we assumed her behavior was only in our home. We'd never had any bad reports

All names have been changed.

from neighbors or her teachers. If we could be patient, I was sure Carol would get through this stage.

Then one day I received a call from the school; the caller said it concerned Carol and that it shouldn't be handled on the phone. The counselor told me that Carol's attitude had completely changed, that there was a serious problem, and that the school recommended psychiatric evaluation.

"Psychiatric!" I cried. The word frightened me. "Isn't that a little drastic?" There's nothing wrong with my daughter; I thought, it's just a phase. I said I'd speak to my husband.

Jim and I talked long into the night. We agreed that she wasn't the Carol we had lived with all these years, but we couldn't believe there was anything abnormal about our daughter. And yet, we had to know for sure. We decided to do what the school recommended.

The real nightmare began with that visit to the psychiatrist. Instead of hearing that we had nothing serious to worry about, the doctor said that Carol should be hospitalized immediately. If not, there was a strong possibility that she could harm herself or someone else. Although he spoke calmly, I felt as if he had hit me. This can't be happening to us. We're a normal family. But he stressed the importance of acting quickly— before it was too late to help Carol. For the first time I feared for my child.

It was the hardest thing Jim and I had ever had to face. I thought back to some of the threats Carol had made in our home—that she would kill her brother if he didn't do what she wanted; that she wished she were dead. At the time, I had ignored those remarks as childish outbursts. She didn't really mean them. But what if... ?

I'll never forget the day we left her at the clinic in Richmond. She glared at us with pure hatred in her eyes. Could this be the little girl I'd rocked to sleep and cuddled in my arms, this angry girl who wouldn't even let me touch her? I didn't want to leave her, but the doctor told us that it would be best not to visit her until they notified us. Suddenly, I felt tired—exhausted. "Is this my fault?" I thought. What did I do wrong? Jim, too, felt guilty. We consoled ourselves that Carol was getting the treatment she needed.

Two weeks later, we got a call from the clinic. Carol had run away. Somehow she had managed to sneak out of the clinic and just disappeared. Anger rose up inside of me. How could they have let this happen? They were professionals, and we had trusted them with our daughter. They told us that the police had been notified, that they would find Carol. Or maybe she would just come home. Oh, God, please let her come home.

But she didn't come home. Weeks went by. The

FBI was notified and still she wasn't found. The rage inside me mounted, threatening to tear me apart. Why couldn't they find one little girl? I learned that the boy she had been seeing was missing, too; they must be together. Surely with two descriptions now, they would find Carol soon. I was angry with everyone—the boy, the rest of the family, and especially Carol. I was mad at God, too. He shouldn't have let this happen. He didn't care about us. I couldn't even pray. What good would prayer do?

As weeks stretched to months, my spirits weakened. I was convinced it was my entire fault. Why hadn't I seen the danger sooner; why hadn't I been a better mother? With all the worry, our whole family suffered. June, Carol's older sister, cried a lot and confessed she had known that Carol had been sneaking out at night after we all were asleep. She hadn't told us then because Carol had threatened her, but now June was filled with guilt for her silence.

My reaction to this news was horrible. I raged and screamed at June for keeping this information to herself. I took it out on my husband, too, never acknowledging that he hurt the same as I. He also felt he must be to blame, and his job was affected because of all the time he missed searching every lead. My tantrums distressed the whole family. The fury inside me was like a cancer, eating away all reason. Finally our son,

Donny, upset by all the arguing, shouted, "Mom, we're still here!" Only then did I realize that I'd been punishing everyone else for what Carol had done. I'd neglected the others, and now our beautiful family was deteriorating.

On the advice of our priest, Father John, Jim and I went to a weekend marriage encounter, where we were able to talk to each other, acknowledge our fears and our grief, and draw close again. For a while things improved.

As the years went by—almost four of them—our hopes withered. Each holiday, I sat anxiously by the phone and searched the mailbox on the chance that I'd get some word from Carol. Maybe she'd remember me on Mother's Day, or perhaps thoughts of our good Christmas celebration might prompt her to contact us during that season. Was she still alive? If so, didn't she know that we still loved her, no matter what happened?

I knew we had to get on with our lives, but how? Each time the news stated that a body had been found, the police notified us, and we had to go to the morgue to see if it might be Carol. Thank God, it never was, yet the experience so shook us that it took weeks to get over it. If we had received word that Carol was dead, we may have been able to grieve and give her up. But not knowing anything sapped the very life out of us. My health failed, and I was hospitalized with a heart problem caused by stress. At home again, and on the verge of a nervous breakdown, I went to see our priest. I was still angry with God, but I didn't know where else to turn. I remember only one thing Father John said to me, "Kris, when she comes back, don't badger her about where she has been. Just accept her and love her."

When—not if—he'd said. Hope flickered again.

Soon after that, I had the chance to go to Spain on business. While there I decided to visit the monastery of St. Teresa of Avila. I'd heard of its beautiful rose gardens and the Carmelite nuns who make rosaries from the rose petals. I needed some beauty in my life again. It was as lovely as I'd heard. I bought one of the rosaries and strolled through the grounds, but the peace I had been searching for would not come. My walk brought me to the magnificent cathedral there. I went in and found myself in front of a huge painting of St. Teresa. I felt totally helpless. We had tried everything we knew and nothing had worked. Clutching the rosary in my hand, I began to speak to the saint. It wasn't exactly a prayer; I hadn't been able to pray for a long time, but she looked so compassionate and understanding in that picture that I began to pour out my misery to her.

"Please, St. Teresa," I whispered. "help me. I don't know what else to do. Please give me a sign. Just let me know if she's alive or dead. We can't go on in this darkness much longer." I don't know if I was expecting a miracle, but nothing happened. And yet, somehow I felt better just by talking to that picture.

I flew back to the States, arriving home late at night from the airport. A note from my neighbor was pinned to my front door. It said that she had some flowers for me that a florist had tried to deliver that evening. The next morning I went next door to claim my gift.

I stared at the flowers—they were roses! A dozen glorious sweet-smelling roses. Could this be the sign I'd asked St. Teresa for? With trembling hands, I tore open the card. Tears welled up as I read the most wonderful words in the world, "Mom, can I come home? I'll call you. I love you, Carol." Oh God, thank You. You do care. Forgive my lack of faith.

After four years of anguish, those last moments of waiting for her call were almost unbearable. A million questions cluttered my mind. Was she all right? Where had she been? What had happened to her? Was she home to stay? Why had she run away? Then I remembered Father John's words, "Don't badger her—just accept her and love her."

"Jesus, help me," I prayed. "I'm so human. I'm not sure I can do this right without Your help. I don't want to chase her away again."

When the door opened and the beautiful young

lady—not the little girl I remembered—walked in, I was filled with a joy I'd never felt before. "Oh, Mom, I'm so sorry," she sobbed. All the pain and sorrow of the past four years disappeared. Nothing else mattered but that Carol was home. With downcast, wet eyes, I said softly, "I'm so glad to see you again."

I held out my arms, and she ran to embrace me. And all I could think was *Thank You, God, oh, thank You. For this my child who was dead to us, is alive again. She was lost, and is found.*

Someone Watching Over Us

DONNA LOWICH

"My eyes are really burning from the chlorine in the pool. I should have been more careful—now they'll be stinging for days." What started out as a minor eye irritation would become a major factor in the course all of our lives would take in just a few short hours.

It was Saturday and the last day of our family vacation together. We had spent the week at the beach near Atlantic City. It had been a great time for all of us. Somehow we had managed to arrange everyone's schedule so that we could be together. My family unit included my parents, my husband, Walter, my almost-two-year-old son, Jeffrey, my sister and brother-in-law, Mary Lou and Ken, and my nephew, six-month-old Kenny.

Our entire vacation had been wonderful; the weather was perfect all week. This Saturday in July was no exception. We swam and talked and laughed all day in the bright sunshine. But as we packed up our belongings from our place by the pool, I blinked and squinted. "Chlorine! I guess I should have paid more attention to how much time I spent in the pool today," I confided to Walter. Past experience had taught me that for the next few days my eyes would sting and feel very irritated; my vision would be blurry.

We showered and dressed for dinner. Dad, always one to speak about his feelings openly, thanked us for the wonderful time: "I am so proud to be your Dad, and I'm very grateful that we spent this week together. I know I had such a great time."

After dinner, we stopped at the city's convention center, where bands were playing and people were singing and dancing. Dad picked Jeffrey up from his stroller and danced a couple of steps with him, one of his favorite things to do. He didn't finish the dance, but instead, he quietly put Jeffrey back in the stroller and sat on the bench right next to him.

"Dad, are you okay?"

"Oh, yeah, I'm okay. I guess I'm just a little tired. It's been a busy day, a busy week." He winked at me and smiled. "Don't look so worried. I'm fine, just fine." That, too, was typical of Dad, never wanting to bring attention to himself, never wanting anyone to worry about him.

"Just the same, please promise me you'll see the doctor on Monday."

He looked at me and hesitated before speaking. I thought he'd be annoyed because he never liked to go to the doctor, and never liked reminders about going, either. Instead, he smiled faintly and said, "All right. You win. I promise I'll go."

I smiled my approval. "You'd better go! Or I'll keep at you until you do!" I teased, not wanting him to know fully the extent of my concern.

"I think I'll head back to the room now," Dad said quietly after listening to the band for a few more minutes. We were surprised because this was Dad's favorite thing to do on vacation: go to the town's band concert, listen to the music, and dance with Jeffrey in his arms.

"Maybe we should all go back to the hotel now," suggested Mom, as she began to gather their belongings.

"Maybe with a little rest, we can go to Atlantic City," agreed Dad. Going to Atlantic City had been a possible destination for our last night of vacation, since it was close to where we were staying.

We returned to our rooms. I waited a while, and went to my parents' room. Dad was sitting on the edge of the bed, encouraging my mother to go to Atlantic City. "I think you should go. I'm a little tired now, but you should go. You'll enjoy it."

Before long, plans were in place: Mary Lou, Walter, and Mom would go to Atlantic City. Ken stayed with little Kenny. I begged off because my eyes were stinging and my vision was blurry. Besides, I thought to myself, "I can stay and watch Dad."

After they left, I waited for just a few minutes, and went to check on Dad. He was sitting in a chair by the door. He was leaning forward, looking down at the floor. That was not like Dad, usually a robust and jovial man.

"Dad, are you okay?" It was hard to hide my concern this time, but I did the best I could.

He looked up at me, gave me a weak smile, and replied, "Just feeling a little upset, that's all. Maybe I had too good a dinner." He smiled his weak smile at me again.

"Dad, I'll be right back." I knew I had to get help, but I didn't want to upset him. I leaned over to kiss him, and I touched his arm; it was cold and clammy.

I ran to the front desk and told the young man on duty that I thought my father was in some trouble. I described the symptoms, and about touching his arm, and the clamminess of his skin. He said he was a member of the city's rescue squad. "I'll be right down to the room," he promised.

I ran to check on Jeffrey. He was sleeping peacefully so I ran back down the hall to Dad's room. "What am I going to tell him?" I worried to myself. "He's going to be upset that I caused a ruckus for no reason."

I knocked lightly on the door, and went in. Dad was

now sitting on the edge of the bed. "Dad, I told the man at the front desk about you. He's on the rescue squad and he's coming here to see you."

Instead of, "Why did you go and do that?" which I expected to hear, I heard, "Okay, thanks." That made me even more nervous. Dad was ill; I knew it, he knew it. We just didn't know how ill at the time. That would become apparent in the next few hours and the days to come.

Before long, the rescue squad arrived, coinciding with my family's return from Atlantic City. They returned almost immediately upon arriving there. Walter did not have a tie, so he was not allowed inside the casino. They took that as a sign that they should come back, which they did, only to find that they had made the correct decision. They came into the hotel room only minutes after the ambulance had arrived.

"Donna! What—?" was all anyone could manage to say. I quickly told them. One of the EMTs approached us. "Your Dad is having a heart attack and needs to be hospitalized. The hospital is about a half hour away. Follow us!"

We quickly made plans for Ken to stay with both Kenny and Jeffrey, and followed the man to the ambulance. The ride to the hospital seemed interminable. The silence was broken with whispered words of prayer lifted to the Lord.

The prayers and silence continued as we waited for the doctor to speak to us after evaluating Dad. The doctor walked into the room, looking grim. "Your husband has suffered a major heart attack," he told my mother. "There appears to be a blockage in the aorta. There has been major damage to the heart muscle."

"What can we do to help him?" we asked, hoping beyond hope that the small community hospital would have some resources that would restore Dad's health.

"We've done what we can for him here," the doctor stated in a very matter-of-fact manner. Then, in answer to the pleading looks on our faces, he said "But I just ended an internship at a specialized heart and lung center. It's about an hour away from here. I can call and see if we can get him evaluated for further treatment there."

More prayers were whispered. Shortly afterward, Dr. Weiner returned, smiling. "It's all set. The ambulance will take your husband tomorrow morning. Once you get there, you'll have to fill out the admission papers," he instructed my mother.

We all breathed a sigh of relief. What a wondrous thing, a doctor at this hospital has connections to a hospital renowned for helping people with heart problems. We weren't past all of our problems, but with this, we overcame a major hurdle. Maybe they could help Dad. We were determined to find out.

After Dad was safely in the capable hands of the cardiologists and nurses at the heart hospital, I had some time to reflect on the past few days. It never occurred to me until then that at some point while I was checking on Dad, my eyes stopped hurting. I clearly saw the miracles formed by the hand of God in the twists and turns of these life-changing events. How else to explain my temporary eye irritation that kept me near my father and then left as quickly as it had come, the young EMT who happened to be on duty at the front desk that night, culminating with the trip to the small community hospital that had as its Emergency Room doctor someone with connections to a specialized hospital that suited our desperate needs?

These may not be what some think of as "major" miracles but, on the other hand, I don't know if any miracle can be classified as "small." However, I am very sure that this series of miracles came together to answer my family's prayers that night and the days that followed. We were given the gift of having Dad for an additional ten months, and we will always be grateful for the extra time that we had to spend with him.

I am also convinced that on that day, and every other day, there is Someone watching over us.

CHAPTER 4

When God Intervenes

Feed the hungry! Help those in trouble! Then your light will shine out from the darkness, and the darkness around you shall be as bright as day. And the Lord will guide you continually, and satisfy you with all good things, and keep you healthy too; and you will be like a well-watered garden...(Isaiah 58:10–11, TLB).

159

All miracles come from God, but there are times when He steps right into our lives to help us with our conflicts, to guide us around obstacles, to hold us in His arms and ease our pain. With this very special kind of healing, God also makes it possible for us to pass on His blessings to others, and this is, perhaps, one of the most beautiful blessings of all.

Every Knee Shall Bow

DIANE M. CIARLONI

My knees were a mess. The pain was so excruciating that I required at least three rest stops to make it up the stairs of my split-level home. My doctor, who said the only solution was a surgery that allowed the cartilage beneath the patella, or kneecap, to be scraped clean, told me the condition most frequently afflicted athletes. That should have eliminated me since I didn't have an athletic bone in my body. I was stubbornly putting off the surgery since it necessitated a three-month-rest recuperation and I couldn't afford to be away from work for such an extended period. Actually, it wasn't just my knees that were in need of repair. My entire life was disheveled, and I was spinning through an horrendous mental and emotional storm. I was searching for relief and not being at all successful in finding it.

One evening, as I labored up the stairs from my office, I heard what sounded like preaching coming from the television. That was strange since neither my husband nor I were church-goers and since I, in particular, couldn't tolerate TV evangelists—or any other kind, for that matter. It seemed to me they preached for a few minutes and spent the remainder of the hour asking for money.

Why in the world had my husband's channel surfing stopped on a Christian station? I hobbled up the remaining stairs to find him in his chair, mesmerized by what was happening on the screen. "What's going on," I demanded.

"Look at this," he answered. "Is this mass hypnosis or what?"

I looked at the screen. Music was playing while thousands of people stood, most with hands in the air, many with tears streaming down their faces, all with a look of peace resting on their features. For the first time in my life, I was witnessing a crusade and, like my husband, I couldn't understand what was happening.

I sat and watched the remaining fifteen minutes of the program, carefully noting when it would be on again.

The Holy Spirit began leaning on me from that moment forward. My birthday was a few days away and I asked my husband for a Bible. He looked at me strangely but complied. He also handed me another package. I suppose he was hedging his bet, just in case the Bible turned out to be a joke.

I began with Genesis and read straight through. Every time a doubt or a question popped into my mind, the Holy Spirit (only I didn't realize it was the Holy Spirit) led me to the scripture with the answer. It was such an amazing experience that I lived in a state of awe for three weeks.

Then, while watching the same evangelist on television, it was announced that he was going to conduct a crusade in my own city. I didn't comprehend what was happening to me but I was determined to go and insisted my husband accompany me.

We arrived at the Convention Center on the appointed afternoon and couldn't believe the panoply of people spread out down the streets, around the blocks, jammed against the doors, sitting on the grass. It was impossible for us to comprehend the situation.

The doors finally opened and we streamed in at the end of one of the numerous lines. Once inside, the best we could do was two seats in the "nose bleed" section. My fear of heights was compounded by my knees so I climbed carefully, sat, and waited.

Music began playing after just a few minutes. All the people around me knew the words to the songs, singing while I silently listened. Some had their hands raised and others were already crying. Four songs later, the evangelist appeared on the stage.

He took the microphone and said, "The Holy Spirit is here and he's bringing healing."

He began calling out healings. Someone, he said,

was being healed of diabetes. Another of a heart condition. I began feeling as if I were participating in a sideshow. I was in full-blown doubt about whether or not I should even be here when he said:

"There's a woman here who has terrible pain in her knees. She's being healed."

I stopped.

"Sure," I thought. "Me and at least five hundred other people with bad knees."

We sat through the remainder of the program and, amazingly, I was moved to tears at certain places. I even found myself raising my hands and looking up toward a Lord I'd ignored for twenty-five years. When the altar call came (I didn't know that's what it was), I rose from my seat to go down.

"You'll never get down there," said my husband, looking at the thousands of people headed for the areas surrounding the stage.

"I've made it this far," I responded. "I think I can get down there."

He stood and came with me. It took a while but we both reached the bottom level and, with more tears and more raised hands, we accepted Jesus.

I didn't say a great deal on the ride home. I felt too full to speak. My habit before going to bed was to wrap my knees snugly in Ace bandages since that seemed to help me sleep. I forgot the bandages that night.

The following afternoon I took the mower from the garage with the intention of mowing the lawn.

"Don't do that," said my husband. "You won't be able to walk when you finish."

I calmly told him I'd be fine. He hadn't noticed the lack of bandages the preceding night.

I began mowing. And I mowed. The front lawn is large but the back is the real killer since it's mostly hillside. That means holding onto the mower handle for dear life while locking my knees to prevent sliding downward. I hadn't mowed the back in several months because of the pain it caused.

I mowed the back.

I finished, put away the mower, and entered the house on the lower level. Taking a deep breath, I walked briskly up the stairs without stopping. I reached the top, turned, went down, and repeated the process. There was no pain.

I kept quiet about the turn of events. My brain told me this was nothing more than a coincidence and the pain would return at any moment. My spirit, however, told me I was that woman the evangelist had referenced.

One night, about two weeks later, my not-always-observant husband asked about the absence of the Ace bandages. I told him what I thought had happened. He was incredulous so I swung my legs over the side of the bed, stood, and dropped into several deep knee bends. There was no pain.

The weeks passed and my pain-free knees began leading me forward. I felt as if I were emerging from a thick fog. My mind and my spirit cleared. My heart came together. My soul righted itself. I had opened the door and Jesus had come in.

That was twelve years ago. I've mowed the lawn hundreds of times and made too many runs up and down the stairs to even estimate the number. Not once has there been the slightest hint of pain.

I was, truly, that woman, and my knees, too, can now bow.

The Ice Storm

BOB BEDORE

New Year's Day 1998, my wife, Pat, awakened with excruciating back pain. Years in nursing had strained her back, causing frequent pain, so I wasn't too alarmed. I figured she would take some pain medication and we would be on our way to Florida for the winter, as planned.

"Bob, I have to go to the hospital," Pat said, pain etching her face. I helped her into our car, packed full for our trip south, and drove twenty-two miles to the Adirondack Medical Center in Saranac Lake, New York. The emergency room doctor examined Pat, gave her medication and sent her home.

"I'm going to lie down awhile," said Pat. While she rested, I did the last-minute preparations for our trip. We'll just get a later start, I thought. Once the medicine kicks in we'll be on our way.

An hour and a half later, Pat cried out. "I can't stand this! Something isn't right."

"Do you want to go back to the hospital?"

"Yes, but I can't walk. The pain is too great."

When the Tupper Lake EMTs arrived, they could not get the gurney down the hall to the bedroom. The paramedics helped Pat down the hall and through the garage to the gurney. I cringed as Pat cried out with each step.

This time the doctors admitted her. To control the pain, they gave her valium with morphine every fifteen minutes, but the pain did not subside. The next day, Friday, more doctors examined her, but still found no cause.

"Why can't anyone find out what's wrong with her? No one has that kind of pain with nothing wrong." I asked everyone within earshot.

"I'm in communication with colleagues in Burlington Medical Center. I'm sure between us we can care for your wife," her doctor replied. "Don't worry."

The Burlington hospital was one of two large teaching hospitals within a 150-mile radius. I wondered if I should have them transfer Pat to that hospital. I felt helpless. Pat always took care of matters like this.

I called our children. Neither son could leave work. Kelly, a corrections officer, was working upstate, and Kurt was in Antarctica delivering supplies. However, our daughters, Cara and Lea, and daughter-in-law, Kelly Ann, were able to come for the weekend. Even though heavily sedated, Pat still complained of excruciating pain. She seemed to lose all track of time, and seldom recognized us.

On Sunday, rain started with predictions of falling temperatures. That night, the rain turned into an ice storm. I prayed the girls would get home safely, especially Cara who lived in Albany, 150 miles away.

Inside the hospital, a storm also raged in Pat, but her temperature was going up, not down. In the days ahead, it spiked to 108 degrees. The doctors ordered the antibiotic Rocefin and moved her into the intensive care unit (ICU). Pat's sisters and her friend, Annie, started calling prayer lines. We all were desperate for answers.

"Maybe Pat should go to another hospital," I said to her doctor.

"There is an ice storm out there. It's too dangerous to transport Pat right now," she replied. "And we are still in consultation with doctors at the Adirondack Medical Center." She was trying to reassure me, but I grew more concerned.

I was afraid to leave the hospital. Afraid something worse was going to happen. In between the allotted ICU visits, I paced the halls, occasionally finding an empty bed and collapsing for a brief, fitful nap.

As the ice storm destroyed forests, homes and power lines outside, something inside Pat was destroying her. "Why can't anyone find it?"

The storm relentlessly made its way across the northeastern United States and Canada, and a storm broke loose inside of me as well. In five days, the doctors had not found the cause of Pat's horrible pain. I was afraid of losing my wife. Like the trees outside, I was falling apart. I knew I was getting huffy with the doctors, but I did not know what else to do.

When the electrical power went off in the Tri-lakes area and the Medical Center personnel turned on their generator, I asked that Pat be transferred to another hospital. I figured a teaching hospital might have more specialists who could identify the problem. In addition to the hospital in Vermont, there was another one in Albany. The distance to each was about the same. The doctors remained reluctant due to the ice storm.

With each cracking branch and power line that went down outside, a bit of my reserve broke as well. Determined to get Pat transferred, I approached her doctor Wednesday morning.

"Pat's been here for a week and she's worse than when she came in. I want her transferred—now!"

"I'm sorry," said Pat's doctor. "That is impossible. The ice storm has immobilized the whole area."

"Will you at least try?"

Pat's doctor called the Burlington hospital, but did not reach it because of power outages. A short time later, the hospital's generator burned up, leaving us in total darkness. No electricity. No generator for backup. Soon the hospital would be as cold as the ice outside.

Heartsick, I sank into a chair beside Pat's bed, certain that all hope was lost. Pat would die in a cold, dark hospital and I was completely helpless to do anything. I wondered if the prayer lines had also lost their power.

"Mr. Bedore, we have been able to reach the Albany Medical Center, and will be transporting your wife there as soon as the ambulance arrives," said a nurse holding a flashlight.

"How? What...?"

"When there is total power outage, state law requires the transfer of patients to another hospital as quickly as possible."

I wanted Pat transferred, but now I worried about the journey. This ice storm was breaking all records. If the ambulance did not slip on the slippery streets, ice-laden treetops could snap off and crash on top of it. I shook my head to chase away the fearful thoughts.

At 6:00 PM, as flashlights and ambulance headlights cut through the pitch darkness, medical personnel began loading Pat into the ambulance. When I learned that one of Pat's nursing friends, Barb Dukette, would ride with her to Albany, I felt better. Just as they were sliding Pat and the gurney inside the ambulance, our youngest daughter, Cara, arrived. She had driven up from Albany. We had no idea she was coming. I was so relieved to see her.

"How are the roads? Is it safe?" asked the ambulance driver.

"Yes, the way I came is clear. It's different from the usual route." With that, Cara climbed into the ambulance with Pat, and they left for Albany. I followed in her car.

Cara was acquainted with the area, as she worked at the Albany Medical Center examining newborn babies' hearing. She drove the ambulance when they got into city, arriving at Albany Medical Center at 9:00 PM Friday. Pat was totally incoherent by the time she reached the Albany Hospital. Apparently, she thought she was out west, sometimes in Arizona, sometimes in New Mexico. She became smart-alecky with the doctors, not at all like the quiet Pat we all knew. However, she did provide some laughs in the scariest time of our lives.

Thirty different doctors examined her and by five o'clock the next afternoon, they had a diagnosis.

"Your wife is in serious condition," said Dr. Allan Carl, spinal orthopedic surgeon and department head. "She has an epidural abscess on her spinal cord. Her only chance for survival is surgery."

There was still the risk of death or ending up a vegetable. I fought down my panic and signed the papers for treatment. Dr. Carl operated on Pat at five o'clock the next morning, ten days after Pat's pain started.

The nine-inch epidural abscess sat directly on her spinal column. The bacteria in the abscess were pneumococci, usually found in the lungs. No one could explain how it got into Pat's spine. If the abscess had burst, she would be dead. God answered our prayers for a safe and successful diagnosis and the surgery, but there was still a long process for healing ahead.

Pat remained in Albany Hospital for nine days. After her discharge we stayed at Cara's house, as Pat still required a lot of care, with outpatient treatment every day.

Pat had graduated from the Albany Memorial Hospital nursing school in 1959, and worked in the profession for thirty years. Now she was the patient, and I was the caregiver. For two weeks, I injected Racifin into an IV through Pat's left arm. When Pat looked at me dubiously, I would say, "Don't bother me." I was confident as I had practiced in the hospital, and I was happy to be able to do something to help her recover. A visiting nurse came daily to change bandages on the fifty sutures in her back and check the drainage tube. In the outpatient center, Pat learned to walk again and go up and down stairs. Still, she had months of recuperation ahead of her.

Some may see an ice storm and a major power failure as disastrous, but for us, it set into motion the making of a miracle.

God's Network

RACHAEL PHILLIPS

In the early morning quiet, I heard my mother's footsteps padding across the cement floor toward my little bed. I could not see Mama because my swollen eyes were sealed shut by infection. A nasty unknown illness had attacked our missionary family in Linares, Mexico, that winter in 1959. I felt a warm, damp washcloth swab my eyes. Little by little my mother's weary face appeared, and my six-year-old heart gave a big sigh of relief.

After a week of high fever and diarrhea, I felt better. I really loved Mexico. My best friend, Maria, and I played house together every day, though she spoke no English and I little Spanish. The happy music that poured from the cantinas across the street every evening made my feet dance. My older brother, Nate, also recovered from his illness, and we once again raided the orange and tangerine trees that grew within the high-walled mission compound. My parents, both ill, managed to stay on their feet and tried to continue the hard work of taking the gospel of Christ to the villagers.

But my two-year-old sister, Jan, was losing ground. I had always envied the blonde, wavy hair that curled around her shoulders. The Mexicans often crossed themselves when they saw her, thinking she was an angel. Now her little white face grew thinner and thinner, and she looked as if she might fly to Heaven any moment. Jan would not eat and lay silent on a pillow most of the time, her eyes sealed shut with the awful pus.

My parents packed for a trip up into the mountains to conduct church meetings in mud hut villages. They hoped perhaps the dryer, cooler air might help Jan a little.

My dad found a secure place for Nate and me in the middle of the twenty or so sombrero-and-serape-clad villagers who crowded into the back of the ancient pick-up very early that chilly morning. Mama carried Jan, wrapped in heavy blankets, to the truck's cab. As usual, my little sister did not move. I almost had grown accustomed to her limp skeletal body, carried around like a rag doll. Daddy revved up the engine. We thumped and bumped and swayed over the rocky, dusty roads, climbing steadily. Much later, my parents told us they thought they would bury Jan in the mountains. They reckoned, however, without God's network.

Back in Indiana, their friend, Etta, suddenly awoke from a sound sleep. For a moment Etta could not imagine why she had opened her eyes hours before her regular wake-up time.

A laser-sharp command burned into her thoughts: Jan is in danger. Pray. Now.

"Leo!" Etta elbowed her snoring husband. "Get up! We must pray for little Jan!"

Her sleepy husband arose with her, and the two clasped hands and prayed fervently for my sister. In the fifties, letters to other countries sometimes took months to arrive, if they were delivered at all. Telephones were not found in Mexican villages. Etta and Leo had no inkling of Jan's desperate situation.

But God did.

My little sister, who had said nothing for days, suddenly stirred on my mother's lap. She opened her eyes and began to sing in a weak but clear voice a song she had learned in Bible school:

God can do anything

Anything, anything...

Mama and Daddy hardly dared hope she would get well. But it appeared Jan would survive another day. And another. And another.

Recently my sister celebrated her fiftieth birthday and many years of ministry as a United Methodist pastor. She is the mother of four adult children.

And, oh yes, she still loves to sing.

A Divine Detour

LYNN SEELY

I had no idea that my decision to live in Scotland for a while would allow God to use me in a dramatic way, but it did.

I was living in the northern part of Scotland in the village of St. Combs. The village had been perched near the edge of the North Sea since 1785. Only a modest cliff overlooking a bare stretch of sand and sea grass lay between my cottage window and the moody sea that— each winter—boiled up furious, frothy white caps and flung howling winds along a chastised coast. In the more temperate seasons, beautiful blue skies counter- balanced the tranquil turquoise swells that licked the sandy shore as if apologizing for its winter wrath.

Two glass bottles of cold milk were delivered each morning to my cozy stone cottage. Each bottle had two inches of fresh thick cream at the top, just waiting beneath a gold foil cap. I'd pour part of the heavy cream into my first cup of hot tea and go outside. I'd sit on the front steps of the cottage in my old fuzzy slippers and faded bathrobe while I watched the darkness fade. Then the sun would gently diffuse the early morning mist and gradually layer the sky in delicate salmon hues.

I would often take long drives in the Scottish Highlands—gliding slowly by sweet heather and lush grassy meadows that were neatly divided by ancient stone fences. The afternoon sun painted the green hill-tops bright gold, while leaving the lower slopes in dark olive contrast. It was always peaceful and beautiful and I never tired of seeing what was around the next bend in the road.

One particular day I was heading home after a leisurely drive in the countryside and although I was near home and had driven this part of the route many times, for some reason I ended up lost. I knew I would need to find a place to turn around, though I wasn't in any hurry to do so. As I came around a curve I saw an accident had taken place. A huge backhoe was on its side. It had fallen off a trailer when the truck driver tried to negotiate the curve. I saw a woman had been injured and was sprawled on the ground. A group of people stood around her, clearly distressed at her condition. I pulled my car over to the side of the road and wondered if I should do anything. After all, I had absolutely no training in first aid and I didn't think I could help. Even so, I felt a need to walk over to the scene. I heard someone say that the ambulance had just been called and was on the way, but I knew the nearest one was in Aberdeen, some thirty miles away.

I knelt down beside the woman. She had a huge gaping wound in one arm that cut all the way to the bone. She had already lost a great deal of blood. No one seemed to know what to do except reassure her help was on the way. I knew she needed more than reassuring words or the ambulance would end up transporting a dead body. I felt a paralyzing dread for the woman. I silently prayed and asked God, "What should I do?" The moment I did, a sure and certain calm came over me and in an instant I remembered a scene from a TV movie where a tourniquet had been used. I knew exactly what had to be done.

I ran back to my car, grabbed an old ice scraper, broke the handle off and raced back to the victim's side. One man in the crowd wore a big red handkerchief around his neck. "I need that—now!" Without hesitating he handed it to me. I soon had a crude tourniquet in place on the woman's arm. I gently twisted the handle—it worked! It seemed like hours, yet it was only ten or fifteen minutes until the emergency crew arrived. As soon as they were at her side, I stepped back. I prayed that the woman would live.

Just before the ambulance left, one member of the crew said, "You know, you probably saved her life." I didn't mention to him that I had no medical training at all and I had only seen a tourniquet being used once in a TV movie.

As I drove home that day I realized if I had not

taken the wrong route I would not have been anywhere near the accident scene.

Two weeks later I went back to the scene of the accident. As I rounded the curve I saw her. She was sitting in a chair in front of her cottage. Her arm was in a cast from fingertips to shoulder. As I walked up to the woman, her puzzled face suddenly brightened. "Well, now, I don't know your name but I know your face." She turned to her husband who had just come out the front door. "It's her! She's the one that bound me up!"

They both believed it was a miracle that she had not been killed instantly. I agreed.

"I think you should know something," I said. I don't have any medical training at all. I said a prayer at the accident scene right after I got there—and I asked God what I should do. It was the answer to that prayer that saved your life. That is how I knew what to do that day."

I continued, "As for the miracle of my showing up, it is more of a miracle than you know. I was on my way home on a road I know very well and yet I somehow managed to get lost. If that had not happened...well, I wouldn't have been there at all that day."

I know there are times when the road I plan to travel on—both literally and figuratively—may not be the road I end up on. God may have a detour planned.

The Girl Who Was Frozen Solid

JEAN HILLIARD VIG

I grabbed my purse and the car keys, threw on my new green waist-length parka, and started toward the door. Mom called, "Jean, aren't you going to take your boots and snowmobile pants? It's supposed to get colder tonight."

I'd lived on a farm in northern Minnesota all my life and was used to cold weather. "I'll be fine, Mom. Just driving into town to meet some friends. It's not that cold."

I was nineteen years old and thought cowboy boots and blue jeans were more appropriate than warm clothing for a night out with friends. Besides, I had no idea that in just a few hours the temperature would plummet to 25 degrees below zero with gusts of 50-mile-an-hour blizzard winds.

Around midnight, after a fun evening in Fosston with my friends, I was driving home in Dad's big white Ford LTD. I usually took the four-wheel-drive pickup,

x

181

but tonight it was low on gas and Dad had said I could take the car.

Heading home, the snow sparkled festively in the beams of my headlights. I decided to take the old country gravel road because it was a few miles shorter than the blacktop. Besides, I had always loved that road. It meandered through a forest of tall pines. Every couple of miles a house or a farm dotted the landscape, but the rest was pure picture-postcard scenery—icy-blue Minnesota lakes, tall trees and the narrow, winding, hilly gravel road.

I didn't see the small patch of ice in the middle of the road because of the new snow. Before I knew what was happening, the car skidded off to the side and the front wheel slid precariously close to the ditch. I tried to back up slowly, but the tires were spinning. When I put the car in forward gear the front tire slipped off the shoulder and the car became helplessly marooned.

I wasn't frightened, but I sure was disgusted! I could just hear Dad's booming voice when he found out what I'd done with his good car.

I knew there was a house a half mile or so ahead, so I got out of the car, slammed the door and stomped off down the road, forgetting my hat on the front seat. I was steaming over the mess I had gotten myself into, and my anger kept me warm for a few hundred feet. The wind forced me to zip up my jacket collar over my nose and mouth. I shoved my hands deep into my pockets and dug into the snow in my pointy-toed leather cowboy boots.

I walked on a little farther and then remembered Wally's place, in the opposite direction. It should be just a half mile or so, I thought. Wally was an acquaintance of my folks and I knew he had a four-wheel-drive truck and could pull my car out of the ditch easily.

As I passed the car, I felt like kicking the tire, but I trudged on. After a half mile or so, I passed a house. It was dark and there were no tracks in the driveway. Probably out of town, I thought. I walked on another half mile or more. The next house was also dark and the driveway filled with snow without a tire track to be seen. (I found out later that both of these families were home that night and that the wind had blown the snow over all the tracks an hour or so before I became stranded.)

I pressed on. The wind whipped and whistled through the pines. My feet were starting to bother me. My dressy high-heeled cowboy boots were not meant for hiking. Why hadn't I listened to Mom and taken my warmer boots?

Where was Wally's house, anyway? I thought it was just over the next hill. I kept walking, but the fronts of my legs, protected only by my thin blue jeans, were aching from the cold. Down another hill. Why had I taken the shortcut? At least on the blacktop there'd be cars on the road this time of night.

I struggled up another hill. Finally, I thought I saw Wally's farm in the distance. Yes! There was the long lane leading to his house. I was breathing harder. And then...I blanked out.

Although I don't remember it, apparently I half-walked, half-stumbled, falling at times, down that long lane. I crawled the last hundred feet or so on my hands and knees, but I don't remember doing that, either.

By now, the wind chill factor was 70 to 80 degrees below zero. Right at Wally's front door I collapsed and fell face forward into the snow. And that's where I lay all night.

The next morning Wally came out his front door just before seven o'clock. Normally he didn't go to work until eight, but thank God, he decided to go in early that morning. Wally saw my body in the snow, leaned down and tried to find a pulse. There was none. My swollen face was a gray, ashen color. My eyes were frozen open. I wasn't breathing.

Wally still doesn't know how he managed to pick me up and get me into his car. He said it was like struggling with a 120-pound cordwood stick or a big piece of meat out of the freezer.

At the hospital in Fosston, Wally yelled through the emergency room doorway for help. He picked me up under my arms and a couple of nurses lifted my ankles. My body didn't bend anywhere.

As they were putting me on a stretcher, one nurse exclaimed, "She's frozen solid!" Another nurse, the mother of one of my best friends, said, "I think it's Jean Hilliard! I recognize her blond hair and the green jacket!"

Mrs. Rosie Erickson, who works in bookkeeping, ran out in the hall when she heard the commotion. She leaned over my body. "Wait! Listen!" A hush fell around my stretcher. "It's a moaning sound...coming from her throat! Listen!"

I was wheeled into the emergency room. Dr. George Sather, our family doctor, was on duty that morning. He was unable to hear any breathing or a heartbeat with his stethoscope. Then he attached a heart monitor, which picked up a very slow, faint heartbeat. A cardiologist said it seemed to be "a dying heart."

"We have to get these boots off! Bring some blankets! She's still alive!" The emergency room sprang to life. My boots and jacket were the only clothing items they could get off immediately. The rest of my clothes were frozen on me.

When they cut my jeans off, the staff saw that my feet were black and there were black areas on my legs and lower back. My feet and legs were swollen. The tissue damage seemed so severe that when my parents arrived Dr. Sather told them that if I did live, my legs might have to be amputated. He wanted my parents to be prepared.

Dr. Sather ordered oxygen, and a nurse suggested trying "Aqua-K-pads." Just the day before, a new kind of water-filled heating pad had arrived at the hospital. Quickly the nurses unpacked one heating pad box after another. Fortunately the only nurse on the staff who knew how to connect them to the special water-filled machines was on duty and she directed the operation. My body was frozen so hard that they couldn't pierce my skin with a hypodermic needle. There was no way at first to give me any medication to speed the thawing process or to prevent infection. But the medical team didn't know what Rosie Erickson was about to do.

Rosie found my parents in the hall. "Mr. and Mrs. Hilliard, do you mind if I put Jean on the Prayer Chain at our church?"

Mom, who was completely bewildered at the scene before her, answered quickly, "Yes...please do!"

Mrs. Erickson hurried to her office and made a phone call to the Prayer Chain chairman at the Baptist church where her husband is pastor. The Prayer Chain was set in motion. The first person on the list called the second. That person called the third and so on.

My heart started beating slightly faster. Even though still far slower than the normal rate of about 72 times a minute, the doctors were overjoyed. Slowly I started breathing on my own.

The Prayer Chain was lengthening. Mrs. Erickson called the pastors of the Lutheran, Catholic, Methodist and Bethel Assembly churches in Fosston. They, in turn, called the chairmen of their Prayer Chain groups, who passed the word along.

During the first hours that the Prayer Chain was underway, my legs and feet, instead of getting darker as Dr. Sather expected, started to lighten and regain their natural color. One after another, the doctors and nurses filed in to marvel at the pinkish tinge appearing at the line of demarcation where the darkness started. (That was the line on my upper thighs where Dr. Sather said he thought they might have to amputate.)

The Prayer Chain spread to the nearby towns of Crookston and Bemidji, and Grand Forks, North Dakota. Soon hundreds, then thousands of people were aware that a young woman had been brought in to the Fosston hospital frozen solid and was in desperate need of God's miraculous healing.

One of the nurses, on her way to get more blankets, poked her head into Mrs. Erickson's doorway and said, "She might make it! Her legs are starting to regain color at the top! And her heart is beating stronger!"

Mrs. Erickson looked up at the clock and thought, The Prayer Chain is in full swing now. God is answering those prayers already. Of course, she's going to make it!

At that moment the whole attitude in my hospital

room changed. Now, instead of "She probably won't survive" the feeling was "Perhaps she'll live, but she will surely lose her legs from the knees down."

Before noon that day I stirred and moaned a word that sounded like "Mom." My mother and oldest sister, Sandra, stayed near my bed, holding, squeezing and patting my hands. "Jean, Jean, wake up! Jeannie, can you hear me? It's Mom. Sandra's here, too. Jeannie, we love you. Jeannie, can you hear?" Around noon I mumbled a few words to them.

All over the area the Prayer Chain was continuing.

By mid-afternoon I woke up and started thrashing in bed. The doctors told me later that I moaned and yelled so much that they were convinced I would have severe brain damage.

All day the nurses and doctors watched in amazement as the blackness in my legs and feet disappeared inch by inch.

By late afternoon Dr. Sather thought perhaps my legs would be saved and that only my feet might have to be amputated. A few hours later he was astounded to realize that perhaps it would be just my toes.

In the end I did not lose any part of my body! Normal color and circulation came back to even the blackest parts of my legs, feet and toes.

Dr. Sather had also thought he would have to do numerous skin grafts where huge blisters covered my toes. But these places healed, too, without skin grafting. Indeed, after watching my body become whole again, I am convinced that a miracle did occur. Even Dr. Sather said, "I just took care of her. God healed her."

The doctors kept me in the hospital seven weeks to make sure of my recovery from frostbite and to lessen the possibility of any infection in my toes. And that entire time I never once experienced any fear. I'm convinced it was the Prayer Chain that kept me calm and filled me with a positive faith that I would be healed.

The night I nearly froze to death was over three years ago—December 20, 1980. Since then I met a wonderful man, got married, had a beautiful baby girl and am expecting our second child in February. My husband, daughter and I live on a farm outside Fosston, and my life is a tranquil, happy one. But there isn't a day that goes by that I don't think about the night I nearly froze to death.

I've become a different person because of that experience. Last winter I joined forces with a civil defense expert, an army sergeant, a highway patrolman, and a doctor from Crookston who is an expert in hypothermia (subnormal body temperature). We give talks to people in different towns and counties around here about winter survival. I tell them my story and point out what can happen when you go out in the winter unprepared for the weather.

I'm surprised I can do this because when I was in high school I was absolutely terrified of speech class. The thought of standing in front of people with all eyes on me almost made me sick to my stomach. But now, I feel none of that. I'm proud to share my story with the hope that I can help even one person avoid the mistakes I made.

I believe this is the reason God spared me—so that I can help other people learn how to survive the changeable and very cold winters.

I've changed in other ways, too. My family and I are much closer now. I appreciate every day I'm alive, I have an enormous respect for the power of prayer. I believe that the Prayer Chains saved my life. Thousands of people I didn't even know bombarded Heaven with powerful prayer requests in my behalf, and against all medical odds I survived. I not only lived, I survived as a completely normal, whole human being without even so much as a skin graft. In fact, unlike most other people who have suffered from frostbite, I now experience no ill effects from the cold.

As one minister reminded me in the hospital when we spoke of the Prayer Chain, we, as God's children, have been commanded to "Pray without ceasing" (1 Thessalonians 5:17).

And I'm sure that was what caused my miracle—all those people praying unceasingly for me.

CHAPTER 5

New Paths to Follow

*Don't cause the Holy Spirit sorrow by the way you live.
Remember, He is the one who marks you to be present on
that day when salvation from sin will be complete....be
kind to each other, tenderhearted, forgiving one another,
just as God has forgiven you because you belong to
Christ (Ephesians 4:30, 32, TLB).*

God heals us in many ways—not only from our physical illnesses, but also from the ways in which we withhold our love from others. He can teach us how to survive our grief and begin a new life. He can make us aware that He is part of that life so that when we are confused or lost we don't hesitate to reach out to Him for help. Out of our suffering can come the greatest renewal we human beings can ever know.

House Call

T. J. BANKS

We sat atop the cemetery knoll, my old friend and I, staring in disbelief at the newly made grave. "What am I going to do, Jenny?" I sobbed, crumpling against her shoulder. "What am I going to do?"

I was thirty-four years old and just widowed, with a three-year-old daughter, Marissa. And I had this horrible, aching sense of suddenly not belonging anywhere, not even in my own home.

The house that Tim and I had bought prior to our marriage—a circa 1918 house that I had loved for its quirks, even while he'd complained about its smallness—had, overnight, become a desolate No-Man's Land. I was wandering around in it like one of those shell-shocked WWI soldiers in a Hemingway novel.

Still, Marissa and I had to live somewhere. So I went over the checklist that Tim and I had been working on before his car accident. We'd already contracted people to do the painting and wallpapering, so I went ahead with scheduling those things. My oldest brother finished up the enclosed front porch, putting up the last few pieces of tobacco-barn wood paneling that Tim hadn't gotten to. I cleaned up the rest of the old bead-board wainscoting and painted the trim in the kitchen.

Better, I thought, once those things had been completed, but it's still not enough. I moved my bedroom up to the third floor, where Tim's absence would, I told myself, not haunt me so deeply. I took down the mini-blinds and put lace panels in their place, hoping to let the light in but, at the same time, to maintain some privacy. I hired a carpenter to build a new stair railing, extra kitchen cabinets, and covers for the old-fashioned, stand-up radiators.

Nice, I said to myself. But, in my heart of hearts, I knew I'd been happier when the whole house was still a work in progress, with barely any wallpaper up and what Tim had scathingly called "garbage-bag brown paint" in the kitchen. He'd been there with us, joking and moving through the various projects with that quicksilver energy of his.

I kept working on the house—changing floors, having the bathroom redone, painting and putting up border on the back porch, and basically doing whatever I could to make both the house and myself feel at ease with one another again. Then, one morning, a good five years after Tim's death, I was painting the kitchen—again—when the truth came to me. Not with any fanfare but quietly and kindly, like an old friend waiting for just the right moment to speak her mind. It's time, isn't it? Truth said, pulling up one of the Hitchcock chairs that I had so carefully saved up for early in our marriage.

Yes, I said, pausing in mid-brushstroke, it really is. I don't want to be here anymore. Not without Tim.

I found a realtor—or, rather, a realtor found me. Lori showed up at my back door one day, canvassing the neighborhood for prospective sellers And I found a house—or, I should say, the house, like Lori, found me. Early one Sunday afternoon, I was scanning the real estate section in the paper when one house in particular caught my eye. The picture showed a white Cape Cod house in the town where Tim and I had grown up. It was very similar to the one I'd grown up in and very much within my price range.

By the end of the week, I was standing in the Cape's wide sunny living room, and I knew (without knowing how I knew) that I had come home. I could see us sitting in this living room, my grandmother's black cat andirons presiding over this hearth as they had over the great stone hearth in her old farmhouse (there'd been no fireplace in our 1918 house)—could see Marissa playing in the finished-off section of the basement on rainy days. There were enough trees on the property to satisfy my tree-worshipping heart and an inexplicable but strong feeling that the house, which had been neglected by its current owners, had been waiting for us.

Oddly enough, my father-in-law, pragmatic soul that he was, wrote me a letter that underscored this feeling. He was living in Arizona now, but, of course, remembered the neighborhood well. "There was one house that always intrigued me," he remarked. "It was on the corner of...." And he pinpointed the exact location of the white Cape, the house that locals still referred to as "the old Clark house."

Of course, it takes awhile to put down roots in any relationship, and this new one that we were entering into with the Clark house was no exception. I tackled both house and yard slowly, trying to get a good feel for what they needed. And there were still things that I had to call experts in for, such as wallpapering, rewiring, and removing the half-dead shrubbery out in front. But I did more of the work here myself, rag-rolling the majority of the rooms in purples, mauve, and creamy yellow, and putting in flowers, trees, and herbs that spoke to something deep inside me. As I painted each room, I, like the walls, became alive and singing with color. Likewise, as I planted Peace roses, rainbow-hued irises, and hydrangea outside, I drew new strength and energy from the ground I was working. In restoring the house and yard, I had found myself again.

It has been three years since we came here. Perhaps the pussywillow tree that I put in a couple of years ago says it best. I have always loved pussywillows—as a sign of spring and for memory's sake, but especially for the old Polish legend about them. According to that legend, some kittens were thrown into a river; and the mother cat cried so piteously that the willows on the bank felt her pain and held out their branches for the kittens to cling to. My tree reminds me of that legend and how, in a very real sense, God called to me, holding out a life-line, and helped me find my way back home to myself.

I Saw the Hand of God Move

JOE STEVENSON

I've always believed in God. But over the years my beliefs about who God is—and what He can do—have changed. It wasn't until my son was gravely ill that I learned you can believe in God and yet not know Him at all.

Know. Knowledge. Logic. When I was younger, those were the words I wanted to live by. As a child I contracted scarlet fever, and this illness ruled out my ever playing sports or roughhousing around. The only real adventures I could go on were adventures of the mind. I read books with a vengeance—Great Books of the Western World, and the volumes of Will and Ariel Durant, and literally thousands more—and out of my reading I formed my strongest beliefs. I believed in logic, in the mind's ability to put all creation into neat, rational categories.

At the same time I was growing up in a strongly Christian family, and so I believed in God. But I insisted—and my insistence caused a lot of arguments—that God Himself was also a Being bound by logic and His own natural laws. I guess I pictured God as a great scientist. Miracles? No, God couldn't and wouldn't break laws in that way. When my family told me that Christianity means faith in a loving, miraculous God, I turned away and went looking for other religions—ones that respected the rational mind above all.

As I became a man, my belief in rationality helped me in my career. I became a salesman for the Bell System, and when I needed to formulate sales strategies and targets, logic unlocked a lot of doors on the way to success.

But other doors seemed to be closed. I felt dry, spiritually empty and anxious. I tried meditation, E.S.P. and so on, but the emptiness increased to despair.

In utter defeat, I turned to God in prayer. His Spirit answered with, "I don't simply want belief that I exist. I want you, your will, your life, your dreams, your goals, your very being. And I want your faith, faith that I am sufficient for all your needs." My despair overcame my logic and I yielded all to Him. But just saying you have faith is not the same as having it. In my mind, I still had God in a box.

Maybe that's why I never thought to pray when my oldest son Frank came home from first grade one day and said he didn't feel well. What would God care about stomach flu? A doctor whom my wife Janice and I had consulted wasn't very alarmed about Frank's illness at first. "It's really not too serious," the doctor assured us, "just a bad case of the flu complicated by a little acidosis. Give him this medicine and in a few days he'll be fine."

But Frank wasn't fine, not at all. The medicine worked for a day or so, but then his symptoms—the gagging, choking and vomiting—came back more violently. His small, six-year-old frame was bathed in sweat and racked with convulsions. We checked him into the local hospital for further testing, but later in the evening our doctor said the original diagnosis was correct. "He's just got a real bad case of it," we were told.

I went to work the next day fully expecting to take Frank and Janice home that night, but when I stopped at the hospital to pick them up, our doctor was there to meet me. "I'd like to have a word with you two," he said, showing Janice and me into a private room.

"A problem, Doctor?" I asked.

"Further testing has shown our previous diagnosis was incorrect. We think your son has acute nephritis. It's a terminal kidney disease..." He paused, and I could feel the blood running from my face. "But we've found that in children there's a good chance of recovery. Your son has a ninety percent chance of being as good as new."

But by ten o'clock the next morning the news was

worse. Sometime during the night, Frank's kidneys had failed. Janice and I rushed to the hospital again.

"X rays show Frank's kidneys are so badly infected that no fluid will pass through them," we were told. "The odds aren't in his favor anymore. If those kidneys don't start working within forty-eight hours, I'm afraid your son will die."

I looked at Janice, watching the tears well in her eyes as a huge lump formed in my throat. I took her hand in mine and slowly we walked back to Frank's room. We were too shocked, too upset to even talk. All afternoon we sat at Frank's bedside, watching, stroking his matted blond hair, wiping his damp forehead. The stillness of the room was broken only by the beeps and blips of the machines monitoring little Frank's condition. Specialists would occasionally come, adjust a few tubes, make some marks on Frank's chart, and then silently go. I searched their eyes for an answer, for some glimmer of hope, and got nothing. When our minister came to pray for our son, I could only cry in desperation.

Late that evening, after Frank was asleep, we went home. Friends were waiting with a hot meal, words of encouragement, and news of a vast prayer chain they had begun. And for a fleeting moment, I thought I saw in Janice's eyes the spark of hope that I had been looking for from the doctors all afternoon.

By the following morning, that spark of hope had ignited a flame of confidence in Janice. "I turned Frank's life over to God last night," she told me excitedly, before we were even out of bed. "I feel a real peace about what's going to happen, that God's will is going to be done."

"God's will?" I said angrily. "What kind of God makes little boys get sick? He doesn't care!" And I rolled over. Peace? God's will? No, little Frank would need more than that to get well.

But my anger didn't stop me from trying to reason with God. All that morning, while Janice kept a hospital vigil, I begged and pleaded and screamed at God, daring Him to disprove my skepticism, trying to goad Him into action.

"Who do You think You are?" I shouted once. "Why are You doing this to my son? He's only six! Everybody says You're such a loving God—why don't You show it?" I yelled until I was exhausted. Finally, convinced my arguments were falling on deaf ears, I took our other children to a neighbor and headed to the hospital, thinking this might be the last time I'd see my son alive.

I never arrived; at least, a part of me didn't. In the car on the way, this Higher Being, this remote Power, this unjust God, spoke to me through His Spirit. I felt His presence, soothing my still-hot anger. And I heard His voice, gentle, reassuring. He reminded me that I had made a commitment to Him, that I had promised to trust Him with my life, my all. And He had promised to take care of me, in all circumstances. "Take Me out of the box you've put Me in," He said, "and let Me work." By the time I parked the car, my heart was beating wildly. I sat for a few moments longer, and uttered but two words in reply to all that had happened: "Forgive me."

By the time I reached Frank's room, I knew what I needed to do as clearly as if someone had given me written instructions. There had been no change in Frank's condition, so I sent Janice home to get some rest. Then I walked over to Frank's bed. Placing shaking hands on where I thought his kidneys should be, I prayed as I never believed I would ever pray. "God, forgive me for my ego, for trying to make You what I want You to be. If You will, heal my son, and if You won't, that's all right, too. I'll trust You. But, please, do either right now, I pray in Christ's name. Amen."

That was all. There were no lightning flashes, no glows, no surges of emotion like the rushing wind, only the blip-blip-blip of monitors. I calmly sat down in a chair, picked up a magazine, and began to wait for God's answer. There was only one difference. For the first time in my life, I knew I was going to get one.

Within moments my eyes were drawn from the magazine to a catheter tube leading from Frank's frail-looking body. That tube was supposed to drain fluid from his kidneys, but for nearly two days it had been perfectly dry, meaning Frank's kidneys weren't working at all. But when I looked closely at the top of the tube, I saw a small drop of clear fluid forming. Ever so slowly it expanded, like a drop of water forming on the head of a leaky faucet, until it became heavy enough to run down the tube and into the collecting jar.

This was the most wonderful thing I had ever seen—the hand of God, working. I watched the tube, transfixed, fully expecting to see another drop of fluid form. In about two minutes, I did. Soon, the drops were coming regularly, about a minute apart. With every drip, I could hear God saying to me, "I am, and I care."

When the nurse came in on her regular half-hour rounds, she could barely contain her excitement. "Do you see this, do you see this?" she shouted, pointing to the collecting jar. "Do you know that this is more fluid than your son has excreted in the past forty-eight hours combined." She grabbed the catheter and raised it, saying she wanted to get every drop, then rushed off.

Within minutes she was back. Grabbing a chair, she sat down next to me and, excitedly, we watched drops of fluid run down the tube. We were both awed at what was happening; for half an hour we murmured only short sentences. "Isn't God good?" she asked me once, and I nodded. When she finally got up to call the doctor, I went to call Janice.

An hour and a half later one of the specialists assigned to Frank's case arrived. Taking one look at the collector, he told us that it was a false alarm, that the fluid was too clear. Anything coming from a kidney as infected as Frank's was would be rust-colored and filled with pus. No, he said, the fluid had to be coming from somewhere else. But I knew—Frank was well again.

By the next morning more than 500 centimeters of the clear fluid had passed into the collector, and it continued as the doctors ran tests and X rays to try to determine its origin.

Finally, two days later, our doctor called us into his office. "Joe, Janice, I think we've been privileged to witness an act of God. All the X rays taken in the last two days not only show no kidney infection, they show no sign that there was ever an infection. Frank's blood pressure and blood poison levels have also dropped suddenly...It is a definite miracle."

And this time I wasn't about to argue. At last I fully believed in a God whose love knows no bounds...not the bounds of logic, not the hold of natural laws. Faith. That's what I now had...that and the knowledge that one's belief in God is essentially hollow if the belief isn't founded on faith.

Alone

LYNN SEELY

I threw everything I owned into my car and set off to see America. I ignored the loneliness that gripped my heart. After all, I was used to it. I knew no one was left who cared about me. I wasn't twenty yet and most of my family had perished. I felt utterly alone in this world.

I decided I wanted to see mountains first. After that, I thought I'd drive to the scorched wilderness out west where certain types of cactus grow thorny-pillars as tall as a three-story building. Then I'd travel to the Grand Canyon's gold and salmon-colored ridges topped by ancient twisted pines. At the bottom a life-giving river wandered in its prehistoric bed. I planned on spending time there, too. Next, I wanted to visit the Petrified Forest. There was evidence that an immense forest once covered the land many thousands of years ago.

Then I'd go see the endless miles of undulating waves of grass that defined the great plains. After that, I'd drive to the west coast because I wanted to swim in the salty turquoise waters of the Pacific Ocean. I planned on embracing the rough back of the giant redwoods in California, and later I'd go see the boundless Big Sky of Montana.

As long as I focused on the wonders of this world, I didn't have to consider the more important issues swirling just below the surface of my thoughts. Every once in a while, if I wasn't careful, I found myself wondering if God was real. It wasn't a casual thought, but a great deep longing that I needed to have answered. Yet I was an expert at pushing the longing away because I was afraid the answer might be "NO."

One day, I drove on a highway in Colorado that took me up into the mountains. I decided to see if I could find a place to pull my car off the road. I was looking for a dirt road that would take me deep into the mountains. I found one. I wanted seclusion with nature. I had food and water with me; several warm blankets and pillows, and I looked forward to spending the night in the mountains. I wanted to see the stars in all their glory and the only way to do that was to stay out here. I followed the narrow road as the sun sank lower in the sky. I drove on slowly, weaving around trees and boulders until I reached an area that seemed a perfect place to spend the night.

I ate my dinner stretched out on the hood of my car, my back against the windshield. Overhead was an opening in the trees that offered me a panoramic view of the Milky Way. I had never seen such a wondrous display of twinkling stars. I saw my very first shooting star streak across the sky that night—then another! It was a thrilling way to be camping out in such an area as this. Finally, the chill in the air was enough to make me head back inside the refuge of my car. As I drifted off to sleep, I again wondered if God was real.

The next morning sunlight danced through the swaying trees and eased me awake. After a morning snack, I decided to go exploring. I took off in the direction of the sun. A short time later I made my way around a jumble of huge boulders and stopped. I was stunned. It was a vast expanse of such extraordinary beauty it took my breath away. Magnificent mountains stretched up—imposing and ancient—silent sentries with brilliant white crests. Each seemed designed to help hold the delicate cobalt sky aloft. An emerald tapestry of pines, still wearing patches of lacy white snow, draped the lower slope of one mountain all the way down to where I stood. Pine boughs waved in a graceful rhythm and gently diffused their pleasant fragrance in the air, while birds that rode their swaying limbs boisterously scolded a warning of my presence. What a beautiful place this was.

Directly in front of me was a frozen lake that beckoned me to explore. It was completely flat except for random mounds of snow that had collected near the shore. A breeze hinted spring was near and had I taken the time to notice, I would have understood the telltale signs that the sparkling mirror of ice camouflaging the lake was melting. Even though I did not know that ice could be thin on a frozen lake at this time of year, had I listened closer I would have heard the lake whisper a warning. Every once in a while a subtle cracking noise in the distance would interrupt the birds chattering, but I paid no heed.

There was something out near the center of the lake that beckoned. It was an odd glaze of pure blue—a reflection of the sky, perhaps—and I wanted to have a better look at it. I answered the flat invitation of the lake as I stepped out onto its smooth surface. Had I grown up around ice and snow, I would have been more wary. However, I was from Florida and the sultry climate I'd grown up in had not prepared me for winter illusions—magical as they appeared—of the north.

I was halfway to the mysterious blue spot when I realized what it was—open water. Instead of being alarmed, I was even more curious. I wanted to get a closer look. I did make a mental note to be careful and not get close to the edge of the opening. But it did not occur to me I was already in a dangerous situation. I didn't know I was only moments away from disaster. I took two more steps and a great cracking noise split the air like a hundred rifle shots.

I stood absolutely still. My heart pounded, as I finally

understood I was in grave danger. No one was within miles of me. No one knew I was here. I was afraid to move. For one brief moment nothing happened. Then all at once the ice gave way and I plunged into the freezing water. I didn't even have time to scream. The shock of the cold water was so severe I involuntarily took huge gasps under water. Even as I struggled I was being sucked deeper. My frantic flailing slowed down to slow motion just before everything went black.

I woke up on top of the ice, coughing up water and gasping in ragged breaths of air. I was about ten feet from the hole where I had fallen through. The first few minutes I lay there as I struggled to breathe, the air around me seemed warm, but soon the cold was biting into me. It took me a long time to get back to my car. Once there I got out of my wet clothing, wrapped blankets around my shivering body, then climbed into the back seat of my car. I soon fell into a deep sleep, too exhausted even to wonder at the events.

The following morning I was stiff and sore. I could not remember how I had gotten out of the lake. I knew I was lucky to be alive. After I had breakfast I decided to walk back to the lake. I wouldn't risk walking on the ice again, but I did want to look at it from the shore. Perhaps then I would remember how I had gotten out.

As soon as the lake came into view, I remembered that as I was sinking in the freezing water yesterday, I felt a presence that I knew was my guardian angel. Just before I blacked out, I heard a voice say, "It is not your time."

I stood there for a long time while I thought about the miracle that had happened to me the day before. My yearning to travel had been about more than just seeing the amazing beauty of this country. It had really been a quest to find out if God was real. The profound experience of the lake did more than save my life. It did more than elicit gratitude. My doubts if God really existed were banished, swept away forever.

Exactly one year later I was given the final gift of that remarkable day.

That evening, after drifting off to sleep, I had a vivid dream. I was at the lake again, on the day I fell through the ice. As if watching a movie, I saw myself walk out on the ice and draw near the place where I would fall in. I noticed all the beauty of the mountains and the crisp clean pine-scented air. Then I became aware of something else. I saw an angel standing close to me. At that moment I understood my guardian angel had always been with me. Not just for that particular day, but always.

I had been profoundly changed by the miracle at the lake. I knew that God was real. Yet it was this final gift that completed the miracle. I was not alone.

Ever.

I Don't Want to Be Angry

KATHRYN LAY

I took a deep breath when the salesperson explained that my order had been lost. I struggled to repeat my verse for the week: "In your anger do not sin...search your hearts and be silent" (Psalm 4:4, NIV).

Each day has been a step-by-step movement toward change since I've made a commitment to not be an angry person. But it's nothing I could have accomplished on my own.

There are support groups for alcoholics, overeaters, and victims of abuse. There are seminars to help people become more organized, less stressful, and a better spouse or parent. But when I realized that, like my father and my brother, I had lost control of my anger, I knew I had to change. But anger can be like a drug, addictive and hard to let go. It becomes automatic. It can be as deadly as a disease.

I knew I needed healing. I needed my angry responses changed. I needed a miracle, an emotional and spiritual miracle.

It took me a while to understand that the anger

wasn't actually a response to anything specific. It was something deep inside that couldn't be changed with a pill or exercise or a new diet. With change came a need for understanding. It wasn't easy to admit that I'd become an angry person and to face the fact that the way I handle my anger is a problem and a bad witness to others of my life in Christ.

As a child, I wasn't an angry person. But as the years went by, I found that my anger came more swiftly and I dealt with it in unhealthy and un-Christlike ways.

I knew it was happening. I felt the rising anger inside, the intense flood of emotions that came when I felt wronged by a person or object or situation. I learned to hide it around those I loved, showing it to strangers...servers, salespeople, and others who made mistakes.

It wasn't until after a confrontation at our bank, the third that year, and the manager called my husband at his job and threatened to cancel our account, that everything came out in a burst of tears and embarrassment.

My husband's reassurances of love and support only made me feel worse. We prayed and I knew that God had brought it into the open to help me destroy this thing inside me that made an otherwise loving, caring woman into an angry, sharp-tongued person. I had lived my life with an angry father, who embarrassed our family in public often with his unreasonable demands and outbursts in stores, restaurants, and on the phone when dealing with business.

Once I accepted that (A) I had become an angry person and (B) it wasn't something that God desired for my life, I found six ways to begin the road to recovery from anger. In six days, God created the world. In six ways, He recreated me and replaced the anger with peace.

(1) The first thing I did was to go to my church and ask for prayer. It wasn't easy to admit my anger, to ask for prayer and support. But it was a first step, and I suddenly had others who told me how they battled the same problem, and many supportive friends to be accountable to.

(2) One way I began to see how anger affects my life as a Christian, how God feels about it, and the peace that can replace it, was by researching the verses in the Bible that dealt with anger.

There were more than I had imagined. After writing each verse in a journal, I went back and rewrote them, adding my insights into what they meant for my life.

In Proverbs 12:18 I saw that the one who speaks rashly is compared to the thrusts of a sword, but the tongue of the wise brings healing. How often I had used my anger to jab at others, cutting bits at a time until I had humiliated them. How much more of a "weapon of God" my tongue became when I used it to bring healing to others when they were suffering, in pain, or in need of comfort, kindness and wisdom.

Proverbs 15:28 (NIV) says that "The heart of the righteous weighs [or ponders] its answers...." Think before speaking. How often I have heard this. The verse continues that "the mouth of the wicked gushes [or pours out] evil." When I am angry, it seems that all my irritation pours out in a flood and I don't stop it or think about it before I let it loose.

Colossians 4:5, 6 (NIV) are two verses I read and took to heart as I dealt with controlling my anger. "Be wise in the way you act toward outsiders; make the most of every opportunity. Let your conversation be always full of grace, seasoned with salt, so that you may know how to answer everyone." (NIV).

There are so many more verses that deal with anger, and others that are encouraging. Ezekiel 36:26 (NIV): "I will give you a new heart and put a new spirit in you; I will remove from you your heart of stone and give you a heart of flesh."

(3) I found a buddy I could call and talk with when losing the battle over my anger. This meant being honest, finding someone who would understand without belittling, someone who would listen, pray, and support me in my recovery. Opening up kept me honest with myself and the Lord.

I also made a pact with myself that if my anger went unchecked and uncontrolled, I would go back and apologize. Like a child returning stolen candy, I found myself holding my temper to keep from having to make such an apology.

(4) I wrote out the scripture verses I found on anger and each week memorized one, keeping it in my heart and remembering it when anger bubbled up. I often think about how the clerk at the grocery store or postal worker must wonder why I mumble to myself.

(5) I made a list of the people and the situations in my life that made me angry during a month. I found that often, after dealing with my father or my mother-in-law or my grandmother, I was quick to resort to an angry word or action the next time someone upset, hurt, or inconvenienced me. I learned that it was necessary to stay away from these people for periods of time, and when confrontations or their actions overwhelmed me, to call my buddy, to read my verses, and to pray for God's peace.

(6) Last, I learned to recognize the signs of my anger. Anger in itself is not wrong. Jesus became angry at unrighteousness and mistreatment of others. There is a time to be angry at injustice and to react—to write letters, find a way to make changes in a bad situation, to form a group of people who will seek God's way in these events.

But, the wild, vengeful anger that results in hatred rather than change is the kind of anger that I must stop before I lose control.

When this happens, the best thing is to remove myself from the situation; to come back to it when I can deal with it in a calm, reasonable way.

I often prayed for a miracle of healing in my life, that the anger would suddenly disappear. But sometimes, miracles happen in stages and come with a partnership with God in an issue.

For so long I was afraid to admit my anger, wavering between fear that others would despise me for it and that it wasn't really a problem. But the peace that has replaced the anger, the ability to see that a situation can be handled calmly with better results, and the knowledge that I will not use my words in a way that is a bad witness to my Lord, has given me a new life. And that is the best miracle of all.

The God Who Heals

ELROY (AL) PLUE

In July 1997, I was scheduled to see a VA doctor who wanted to perform exploratory surgery on me in order to pinpoint the numerous health problems I had been experiencing. The doctor I was scheduled to see had unexpectedly gone home, so instead, I saw the assistant surgeon.

After a casual conversation, he asked me, "Have you ever asked Jesus into your life?"

Startled by his question, I answered, "I've been looking for a church but haven't found one yet."

"You don't need a church to have a relationship with God," he replied.

"How do I do that?"

"Ask Him to come into your life, and He'll begin to direct your footsteps," he smiled.

That night I went into my bedroom, dropped to my knees, and said, "God, I hope You're listening because I sure want this to work. You see, I just can't live like this anymore."

I spent the next few hours reviewing my life and

recalled how I had messed up my children's lives, my marriage of twenty-eight years, and myself. "God, I need help. Please send me somebody. And God, if You can't help me, I don't want to wake up in the morning."

Two days later a business associate outlined the message of salvation to me and asked if I wanted to invite Jesus into my life. I responded, "Yes!" I became born again as I repented of my sins and accepted Jesus as my Savior.

One month later during a church service, I fainted. Although I tried to get up, I fainted three more times. Foaming at the mouth while being taken to the hospital by ambulance, I remember hearing the medic say, "I can't get a reading. Is he dead?"

Once at the hospital, the doctor immediately started an IV. He was bewildered as he looked at my test results. "You should be dead. You don't have enough electrolytes in your system to be alive!"

The next day a doctor was reading the X rays that were taken at the VA hospital. He then sent me to see another doctor. Getting off the elevator, my heart sank when I saw the sign on his door: Byersdorf and Gates: Cancer Surgeons.

When Dr. Byersdorf put my X rays on the screen, he asked if I had seen the test results and if I knew what they meant.

"No," I said, wondering what news would follow.

He then explained that I had colon cancer and lymphoma cancer in my chest.

"What does that mean?"

"You need to be operated on immediately. Without surgery you have approximately ten days to live."

Shocked, I asked, "When do you want to operate?"

"First thing tomorrow morning," he said. "Go home and tell your family your situation." Then he added, "Because of your poor health, the odds of living through this surgery aren't good."

"What are my odds?" I wondered out loud.

"Less than twenty percent."

"Why have the operation then?" I asked.

"You'll die without surgery!" he said. "At least, if you're operated on, you'll have some hope. Go home and try to muster up a good attitude."

Taking his advice, I went to the home of my estranged wife. I gave her the doctor's report and asked her to tell the kids. I then went home to be alone. In my bedroom I began to talk to the Lord.

Being a new Christian, I had learned a few spiritual truths. I knew from reading the Bible that when Jesus went to the cross, He provided both salvation and healing for me, and all I had to do was to ask Him to be healed.

I poured my heart out to God. "Lord, I know there's a time for everyone to die. If my time is up, I'm prepared for that; but if I don't have to go yet, I don't want to. I want to see my sons married and to see grandkids." Thinking of my future I added, "I want to get my house in order and give restitution to my family instead of the heartache that I've caused them."

At 3:30 in the morning, a bright light awakened me. A blue haze surrounded the light and slowly moved from the corner window toward me. I said, "God, is that You?"

The light penetrated my chest and warmth flowed through my body. The light rested awhile; and when it began to withdraw, an emotional weight lifted off me. The light moved back to the corner where it entered the room and seemed to hover there as if to say good-bye.

I laughed and cried. I knew God had touched me.

I fell asleep and awoke the next morning full of exuberant joy. Walking back and forth through my apartment, I repeated, "Thank You, Lord."

Checking into the hospital, the staff thought I was either in shock or just plain nuts. "What a great attitude you have," they said. Little did they know that the doctor would only have to do a "mop-up job." God had already done the real work.

Prior to the surgery, the doctor told me I would need a minimum of two weeks of round-the-clock monitoring in the intensive care unit and then three to five weeks of recovery.

When I awoke in intensive care, the nurse said, "If I didn't know better, I would say you never had surgery. All of your vital signs are normal!" The next afternoon I was moved out of the ICU unit. Every time the medical staff checked my vitals, they left my room shaking their heads.

Several doctors accompanied Dr. Byersdorf when he visited me. He described the lymphoma as an old cow pie that got too much sun. He said they scooped it up, did some trim work, and felt that they had gotten all of it. The colon cancer was also successfully removed.

Later, a nurse came in when I was up and said, "You shouldn't be out of bed!"

"But I have to go to the bathroom," I explained.

"You've got to be kidding," was all she could say.

My doctor frequently told me that I was the talk of his colleagues. Some said my recovery was a miracle; others said it was medically impossible.

The doctor soon asked, "Do you want to go home? We're not doing you any good here. All of your systems are normal, and you can rest at home." I was released from the hospital three days after surgery.

Initially, I was told that it would be at least two months before I could drive a car. I drove in four weeks. The doctor said it would be six months before I could return to work. I went back to work in two months.

Before starting a year of chemotherapy, I was told I

would lose my hair, be sick, and lose weight. I had no sickness, kept all of my hair, and gained fifty pounds.

Five years after my surgery and after being told that I only had ten days to live, I am still going strong.

A Note from the Editors

This original book was created by the Books and Inspirational Media Division of Guideposts, the world's leading inspirational publisher. Founded in 1945 by Dr. Norman Vincent Peale and his wife, Ruth Stafford Peale, Guideposts helps people from all walks of life achieve their maximum personal and spiritual potential. Guideposts is committed to communicating positive, faith-filled principles for people everywhere to use in successful daily living.

Our publications include award-winning magazines like *Guideposts, Angels on Earth, Sweet 16* and *Positive Thinking,* best-selling books, and outreach services that demonstrate what can happen when faith and positive thinking are applied to day-to-day life.

For more information, visit us online at www.guideposts.org, call (800) 431-2344 or write Guideposts, 39 Seminary Hill Road, Carmel, New York 10512.